Human in Person

One Life to live

Dr N Prabhu Dev

PARTRIDGE

ISBN: Hardcover   978-1-4828-7386-3
             Softcover   978-1-4828-7387-0
             eBook   978-1-4828-7385-6

Print information available on the last page.

To order additional copies of this book, contact

Partridge India
000 800 10062 62
orders.india@partridgepublishing.com

www.partridgepublishing.com/india

Life is a dream for the wise, a game for the fool and a comedy for the rich and a tragedy for the poor.

I have made an attempt to portray life as you and I live and believe. This is purely my perception. I may be right or I may even be wrong. You may agree or agree to disagree. I believe that Life is a game. The Game of Life is not the same as a game of chess as chess is played in the conventional way. Life is full of surprises.

Life is a complex case of cellular automaton starting as a zygote- a unified product of the sperm and the ovum ending up with some trillion cells which are biologically active. Life has to be lived forwards and can only be understood looking back wards - what are called as experiences. What one undergoes is the experience. Life is full of dualities.

I often think of the distance that I have travelled so far and how far I am required to go and also how I go about it. I give a special thought about my strengths and my weaknesses. It is theses that decide the quality of my life. I also think a lot about if any change of gear is required in the way I live.

We sleep, we eat, we laugh, we cry, we breed and we die! Is that all in life or is it something more? I believe that one should confront to change. Otherwise it is static. Only when I distance myself from an issue I am able to see all the sides without any bias. You will not become ugly by calling someone pretty.

As I have alluded to before the life is full of dualities. It is astonishing to know that 90% of life is only a reaction to what happens to you. Actually what happens to you is only 10%. You have to learn to give up your ego and forgive. Forgiveness does not make you any weak but reduces the luggage you are carrying. The life becomes smooth instead of a roller coaster. Move on in life. Do not trust those who have betrayed you in life again. Do not go by what others show you because they actually hide what they are.

I have realized that we always see more virtues in us than what we actually have. The good and bad within us is what we fight with in ourselves. The outcome of this battle fought with in us decides the quality of life. It is not the battle we have to fight with those who do not see eye to eye with us or think differently from us. You don't have to be wrong for others to be proved right.

The basis of Science is facts. Science pursues truth. The facts should be tangible, verifiable and reproducible. Science is not an assumption or presumption. Be kind and gentle, be just, be reasonable are the basic tenants of all religions and philosophies. So be good and do well. Do to others what you would want to be done to you. Your thoughts are what the mind peruses. Thoughts are what you have been practicing.

The young are rough and tough and I am always tender and kind to their deeds. I think of my youth and that makes it easier. As one ages I feel sympathetic and compassionate. I have practiced to be kind and tolerant with the weak. I do not like anyone stronger than me and to confront them. If I have to I believe in the combined strength of the community and the like minded-simple and straight forward.

I believe that whatever bad that happens is not permanent. Good things will be waiting to happen. Life always gives a second, third and many more chances. It is never too late to correct the relationships. It is a fact that wherever there is a will you always find the way. If there is no will you will find excuses.

I have found that decisions taken with kindness in the heart are always right. It does not make you suffer the pain you have to. You are never dressed fully unless you wear a smile. An affectionate hug, a smile, a pat on the back will go a long way in making life easy and beautiful. It doesn't hurt to smile, or be kind, or extend a helping hand.

The ills of life are cured by death. Death executes life. The only constant thing in life is change and be perceptible to the change. It is always said that if you don't think of the past and do the rectification and course correction you are likely to miss the future. One thing is certain that life goes on.

I have wondered why the nature on occasions is so unkind, why are the tsunamis', the earth quakes, disasters, flooding etc are forced on the humanity. Is it to show who is more powerful- God or we humans. Why at times the nature is so chaotic? Or Chaos is it the law of nature? Life is chaotic! Is it not that, Chaos in life makes the life so beautiful! Is Chaos the opposite of monotony? Is monotony the same as orderliness? I am so much confused about the subtle ways of life, the chaotic life and too much of orderliness in life.

To think of it the anger, fear of the unexpected, love is all the outcomes of chaos. These are powerful emotions. We always conjure of Falling in love. No one has ever of Raised in love. Once you fall in love it is a torture to disengage from love, more so if you are the one wanting to continue. Yes the world is cruel so be it. Learn to rise in love.

If a man dedicates his life to good deeds and the welfare of others, he will die unrecognized and unremembered. If he exercises his genius in bringing Misery to many his name will echo through the millennia for a lifetime. Infamy is always more preferable to ignominy. Yes this is my experience in the university I had the privilege of being the Vice Chancellor. The lesson is this. Allow one's self to become shackled by mediocrity. Yes the mediocrity wins. So what!. Let your grasp be more than your reach.

In my simple life I have taken very little but have offered far more than one can imagine. Sometimes I am filled with woe to think that no one in this blighted millennium has the wit to see the scope of my services and sincerity. I have been made to feel that no good deed has gone unpunished- and no evil deed has gone unrewarded-So be it! Society is bad –still do good.

Change the person in the mirror before we decide to change someone else. For by changing ourselves, others will follow. Never let a weak moment take away from you all the strong ones you had.

I have no regrets in my life. I am myself and I am proud of being myself. I am back, and better than ever! Back from the turmoil of university life. I do, what I want to because it is who I am. Anything else is a lie and if there is one thing I can say of myself, it is that I will never compromise who I am. I am truly alive. I am no fish to go with the flow. That's the only way I know how to live. What else is there?

Strong will rule and the weak will submit. It is their destiny. The weak are so submissive that they are not even aware of their inevitable doom. Learn to read not only the lines but more importantly in between the lines. It is not just the Art of living but also living unrecognized uncared and unloving.

Law is the ultimate weapon the weak have against the strong. I believe in law as power for all. The weak shall inherit the earth!!! The law will not allow it! The Strong has the right to Do What They Can, And the Weak Suffer What They Must. A society that protects the weak from the strong must also protect the stupid from the smart. There are two kinds of submission: submission to superior force and submission to superior truth. The first is weakness and the other is strength. Being submissive is NOT something that you do with an abusive man.

Human in person

Bright and beautiful,

Dark and ugly,

Black and Beautiful.

Life is full of dualities and this makes it beautiful.

Every day we face conflicts and contradictions. Sometimes we call them problems or roadblocks. Conflicts are because of contradictions within us and with others.

Say for example Democracy vs. People making bad choices. Democracy is not perfect and not good for every society. The problem is what system works better I do not know. I know for sure that Democracy is the best for us! Am I sure? No not really! Enjoy every day vs. live careful, healthy lives. This one is a draw

Let me start with a question! All of us are individually wise and fine. But collectively something goes wrong. From wise we become otherwise. Is it because that you are weak that you are overwhelmed by others. Are we in harmony with ourselves? We will always say somebody else is making us unhappy.

The whole of your life is a procession of several adjustments and alignments that you are making within yourself as well as outside yourself, so that you may not clash with anything in this world. I strongly feel that the old adage- survival of the fittest has become survival of the Cruel or survival of the mighty sinner!

What is life without conflict? It is boring, it is complacent and there is no growth! It is dull without propelling tension. Isn't that a human paradox? While conflict can irritate, it can also beckon. While conflict can bring out the worst in people, it can also bring out the extraordinary. While conflict can make us resist, it can also expand our understanding. While conflict can divide, it can also unite.

Why can't life be simple to live? The world lives on dichotomies and dualities like Rich and poor, peace and war,, Believers and non believers, Hindus and non Hindus, Christians and non Christians etc.

We have the ideologies like Democracy vs. Dictatorship. Communism VS socialism VS capitalism etc. well communism is disappearing even in its so called strongholds.

One should always have it in you that you treat the other with dignity and respect. One should extend what one would want for himself from the other. The strong dominate the weak. The weak has the same right to live peacefully as the strong. This is what the god has ordained! This does not mean for a moment that you have to play safe. There would be No war if all were to play safe!

Live with passion and make life a passion. Do you rock the boat? Or do you go with the flow. Is it wrong to be ambitious? Is it wrong to pursue your ambition with passion? When will I ever find answers to all these dilemmas! Are you sure that the currents will take you out of the storm? Or if you rock the boat what are the chances of getting drowned? Well there are no pre set rules. The life has to be lived forwards and will be your experiences. This is not a game of Chess.

Nothing succeeds like success! Well what about Failure? Can one always succeed and never fail? Failure is the stepping stone of success. If you understand this you will be able to look at both success and failure with more detachment. Are you afraid of failing? Do you fear Failure? Are you afraid of rejection? Do you have a fear Psychosis? Do you fear alienation? Or are you afraid of getting caught and public admonition and humiliation! Well there is no end for the innumerable ways the fear can hit you. Convince yourself that you are not going to be cowed down! You will fight without fear for all that is worth fighting for!

Physical hurt and pain, hunger are basic issues of life. Life will teach you the level one has to fight for one's own safety and be fed sufficiently. In Life never regret anything that has made you smile once.

Courage is not the absence of fear, but rather the judgment that something else is more important than fear.

- Ambrose Redmoon

Courage is resistance to fear, mastery of fear - not absence of fear.

- Mark Twain

Security is mostly a superstition. It does not exist in nature. Avoiding danger is no safer in the long run than outright exposure.

Life is either a daring adventure, or submission to the strong or nothing.

Above quotations make it clear that courage and fear can coexist. Do they complement each other? May be the person becomes more judicious. Or maybe it is wise to be judiciously courageous and know the limits and have the ability to say- this far and no further! Be aware about Fight or flight! Keep both the options and be judicious. It will not be a problem and one can live through these situations and say yes I have! Learn to face fear judiciously. If you only get used to flight response you will never be able to face fear and stand up to it.

The highest courage is to dare to appear to be what one is. You should allow yourself the luxury to catch the glimpses of your own greatness. Mirrors just reflect!

Which is original-Newton or the apple?

The story of Newton and the falling apple is undoubtedly the best known anecdote in the entire history of science. Isaac Newton saw an apple falling from a tree. It was the apple of his eye. That simple incident caused him to wonder why apples always fall. Isaac Newton explained the workings of the universe through mathematics. He formulated laws of motion and gravitation. Isaac Newton used three laws to explain the way objects move. They are called Newton's Laws of motion. There are three of them.

Yes life goes on. Earn respect and respect others as you would want them to do to you. Respect cannot be demanded. Be honest to you first and to your work, to others who are with you. It is highly appreciated. Be loyal to those who are to you. Loyalty is rewarded in terms of return of loyalty. The exceptions are there in the history and one can experience the absence in one's own life. In Life never regret anything that once made you smile.

Life and death – a riddle so real but never was the riddle solved. Centuries after centuries, birth after birth and death after death, we are nowhere near solving the riddle. Life is a journey. Death is the destination. Ensure that you travel this journey in a way that you are useful to others and be true to yourself.

Life is a sum total of what happens to you and how you react to it. Life is what you got from your parents and that which you pass on to your children. You cannot choose your parents.

If you could choose your kids there should not have been so many differently-abled or disabled children with so many deformities sometimes making the lives of parents and children themselves miserable.

Life isn't about waiting for the storm to pass. It is to swim against the tide and winning. Life is also swimming with the tide to conquer in another day. Do not perish facing the storm. Storms are not permanent. Life is to choose when to call off or take a step backwards to take two steps forward later. Enjoy what you want while you endure what you have to.

I enjoy my walk in the morning. I practice meditation. No I do not go to temples to pray .I pray in the small pooja room at home. I enjoy listening to music – light music I also enjoy classical music rendered by the legends-Bheemsem Joshi, Chaurasia. Pandith jasraj, and the like. I like simple poetry and I have penned a couple of them.

Does One live only to die. The life is complete with death after birth. There are no rebirths in between. Life after death is a matter of hypothesis and speculation. There is no confirmation on rebirth. Hindu philosophy believes in Karma and rebirth depending on your deeds in the present life. There is no one who claims to have been born again. Even in the philosophy of karma you are not assured that you will be reborn as a human being. It depends on your deeds; No one in the present life has any iota of advance information on your kind of future birth. Anyways it is said that one can be reborn as any one of the several thousand species on earth. All ifs and buts!

From the very second you are born; you are inching towards your end. Time and tide waits for none! Is it wise to only to waste the present life thinking about mundane things? Yesterday is past and cannot be claimed. Tomorrow is yet to come! One presumes it will come! But it's not in your hands. Today is the present and live. Act now.

It's not wrong to plan the future. It is prudent. You can make decisions can be with the kind of future you can afford. Be useful to the society and the community that has nurtured you. It is not important as to how long you live . What really matters is how you live! Life is not just eating, breeding, crying and dying. There is something more. Live a useful life.

Do what you enjoy. Do it with passion. Many times we live doing things we never enjoy. Worse – we do things that hurt others and us. Regret is what you will be left with. You can undo some of the things. Not all! Some actions are irreversible and so are the results. At the end you want all the glory and you will not want any of the wrongs you have done. You think you earned a place in the heaven.

Remember that that the company in the hell is good with a quiet few like us there. All of us with highly developed art of forgetting the wrong deeds done but refused to accept. I remember the story of a Vice chancellor of a university after his death stands in front of god telling his woes and the torment he had to go through. God as he knows everything tells him that he has already suffered enough and he has paid his dues and allowed him to go heaven.

There stood another Vice-chancellor who was VC for two terms. The VC was mighty pleased that the previous VC made his way to heaven! He thought that as he was a VC for two terms he has reserved his right to go not only to heaven but straight to god's house itself. But god sent him to hell as he thought the VC would be better off in the hell as he was so much used to suffering. Strange are the ways of god!

Tsunamis, tornados, and earthquakes - all disasters! Are all these disasters were waiting to happen because of human misadventures? Or Is it the way god punishes us for the wrong deeds we have heaped on the nature? Is god so calculative? Is he business like? Do wrong and have a disaster as a compliment.

Does god love? Is god compassionate? Is god powerful? All these are sensitive issues and require to be handled carefully! Why is he allowing the evil to triumph and only to unleash a punishment in the end! Is there a reward for the good you do! If there is one why does it have to come in the end when it does not matter! I have no answers yet!

The evil is all in you and me. If he were to decide to eliminate all evil he will have to do something radical. The world will have to go! There is so much of evil! The world lives in dichotomies! World needs evil to coexist with good as birth needs death.

There is a popular perception that that we let the life drag on – days to weeks to months and years- finally to a wasted life! It is often said -time flies, then why this drag? May be it is the way we live that drags life to its inevitable end1! Does time really fly? When one is happy you find the years to be months, months to be weeks, weeks to be days, days to be hours and hours as minutes! Amazing! When you are sad or unhappy or in some trouble the reverse happens. Amazing! Time is a great healer or is it? Yes the memories fade and one is left with loneliness!

I, me and myself – Is all that matters. If you're confused by the words you're not alone!

Who am I?…

I am the CEO of my life." I" internalized in the "self" becomes me. What the individual is for him. Me" disciplines the "I". Self is one's own experience of perceptions, emotions and thoughts. Self seeks to describe essential qualities that constitute a person's uniqueness.

The self is a complex and core subject in my life. Self Image does not necessarily have to reflect reality. Self is viewed in three dimensions Physical description of the personality is the first dimension. One's role in the society marks the second dimension. Personal traits form the third dimension.

Self esteem is the extent to which you love yourself or trust yourself or how much respect you expect from others. Self esteem always involves a degree of self evaluation. Self-worth is "the sense of one's own value or worth as a person. There should not be a mismatch between sif esteem and self worth.

Self-respect is the most crucial aspect of one's life. If you do not understand how to appreciate yourself and your worth, how do you expect others to? Life is too short to maintain toxic relationships. In order for yours to flourish, you need to work on yourself first. Don't expect anyone to love or respect you if you don't fully love yourself first. Respect yourself enough to walk away from anyone or anything that no longer serves you, grows you, or makes you happy.

When everything else in the world fails you, you will always have your self-respect to fall back on. How you feel about yourself affects every single aspect of your life. Learn to accept the love you deserve. The most powerful and influential factor in your life is your own self perception. When there is no enemy within, the enemies outside cannot hurt you" -Les Brown

Personality

Personalities that are more competitive, outgoing, ambitious, impatient and/or aggressive are labeled Type A- Type A personalities have a greater chance of developing ischemic Heart diseases.

Contrast to those of Type a - Relaxed, suave, easy going persons are Type B and are noted to live at lower stress levels.

Am I the root cause of all my sorrows! There is the self, there is mind and there is soul. We should triumph over I. Then there is harmony - Harmony within oneself, with others and with nature.

Living is not easy. Indeed not. There is always something missing always something we are running after, always something that we seek, want, need and desire. Life is a journey filled with lessons, hardships, heartaches, joys, celebrations and special moments that will ultimately lead us to our destination- the unresolved riddle!

I always pray- Forgive, O Lord, my little jokes on you, and I'll forgive you for the big ones on me. Honey is sweet and precious even if it is spread over a thorn. You know the thorn hurts and you have to have the honey. So lick it carefully. It is not the retirement from the world but what matters is the world should feel sorry that you have retired. The world was here before you. The world does not owe you anything,

In life all of us have an unspeakable secret, an irreversible regret, an unreachable dream and an unforgettable love. Miracles happen every day in every one's life. We are blind not to see them, not recognize them and not to perceive them. So we don't for a moment thank the kindness of the provider of the miracles. A hearty laughter, face of a child, beauty of flowers, the enormity of the sky, the tides in the sea, so many things make life so much enjoyable. Have time for yourself before you spare for others.

Life after the journey is completed, life is in heaven/ hell. Are you sure? I am not! No one to vouch because nobody has returned from there! Someone asked me recently what I would do if I knew I had just one more year to live — and then, just one more month or week or day. In truth, none of us can ever know just how many days we are left with. It's not so much about the number of days or hours I have with my friends and loved ones; it's the depth, warmth and integrity of the relationships I build with them during the time we spend together. This is life-long in short.

Humility.

Have no pretensions; be upright, straightforward. Serve your teacher in true obedience, keeping the mind and body clean, tranquil, steadfast, and master your ego. I have vivid memories of encounters with people whose voices or words have moved me over the years. Words have enormous power. Words have a real impact on thought and attitude. They can make us erupt into laughter or bring tears to our eyes. They can influence, inspire, manipulate and shock. They can build and destroy. Some words have different effects on different people. One such word is humility. It is one of those words that are seldom in neutral gear.

Some, like me, love the word and all it stands for. Some almost fear it and interpret it synonymously with lack of self-confidence or timidity. Humility is modesty, lacking pretence, not believing that you are superior to others. Humility is also a meta-virtue. Happiness remains the most cherished yet elusive of all human desires.

On the highest throne in the world, we still have to sit only on our own bottom. Humility is perfect quietness of heart; it is to expect nothing, to wonder at nothing that is done to me, to feel nothing done against me.

We often confuse humility with timidity. Humility is not out of fear. Humility is all about maintaining our pride about who we are, about our achievements, about our worth – but without arrogance – it is the antithesis of arrogance. It's about a quiet confidence .It's about being content to let others discover the layers

of our talents without having to boast. It's lack of arrogance and not lack of aggressiveness in the pursuit of achievement.

You will shun conflicts and win peace! All of us have a tendency to believe what someone else has said- may not be directly to you. You hear it from someone else and the thing would have got twisted and what is presented to you is what that someone else thinks of you.

I have heard of a well researched statement. A teacher asked a student to write the map of India and submit. One student did write the correct map of India. Other students copied what the student had written one after the other. Finally when the last of the students copied the map had undergone unbelievable changes the map of India had become the map of Australia!

Moral of the narration is that when the ill spoken words would have undergone metamorphosis to something else. Do not go by what is conveyed to you. You can talk to the person directly and solve the issue once and for all.

I always pray to the almighty to keep me reasonably gentle and give me the ability to absorb the criticisms in a sportive way and not get into a brawl with those who criticize. Well am I a monk? No I do not really like monks and saints. Believe in yourself and be humble. Show humility and not false modesty. Be frank and fearless. Be sure that this is not a free license to talk rubbish. Make your point in a gentle and a congenial way. Do not be passive. Take a stand! Recognize the merit even in unlikely places or people. When the merit or the skill is noticed or recognized have the courage to tell them loud and clear.

Humility is what you have with god! It is to understand that we are not god. It is the "Knee mail" that works with god! Kneel in front Him and he will lift you! Contribute to the community's good even when you are not asked! Do it for the combined good. Serve with kindness without expecting any award or reward!

Service has to be given out of free will. There is no element of force or coercion. One who has received and the one who has given are supremely happy. There should be no feeling of guilt or insolvency in the mind of the one who has received. One who gives should not have any sense of pride or expectation of a surrender of the one who has received .One who has received is not a beggar and because you have given it you are not a god!

Life is what you make of it. Beauty lays in the beholders eyes. If I behold the beauty in you, I behold the beauty of life. Let go the past. Let not past decide your present- be free of ego and hurt, Be free of revenge. It is never too late to bury the past and make a fresh beginning. Life is beautiful and it is up to you to make it that way. Some people say and I quote "it is my life and I will do with it as I please'. Yes but don't spoil your life.

Don't walk behind me; I may not lead. Don't walk in front of me; I may not follow. Just walk beside's me and be my friend-

The present is now, today. This is the truth! The present is the only thing that exists, the only thing you are ever conscious of. The future does not exist until it becomes the present. There is no tomorrow until it becomes today. Chicken first or Egg first / Egg first or Chicken first' and one cannot be without the other. The riddle is real and has never been solved. Does anybody own the Time? The only thing constant in life after birth is death. What is the aim of life- only to suffer and die or only to enjoy and die in grace or disgrace?

Ralph Barton, one of the top cartoonists left this note pinned to his pillow before taking his own life: "I have had few difficulties, many friends, great successes; I have gone from bed to bed, from house to house, visited great countries of the world, but I am fed up with inventing devices and to find the answer- why am i here?

Whoever is reading this -Enjoy Life -Don't be scared -Keep your heart and mind wide open -Believe in yourself and others -Be happy -Don't care what others think -Put a smile on your face and show the world what you can do.

India was the first to think of globalization through notions like vasudhaiva kutumbakam, the poet says, pointing towards world harmony."Economics is important, but economics is like the canvas behind the painting. You can't have the painting without it, but it is not the painting.

About Life

I am, because the earth is, because the air, fire, water are, because our ancestors are. Everything we are is because of that inheritance."- Lord Byron

Chicken first or egg! The gulf is yet to be bridged. The various concepts are ever confusing and have further widened the gulf. Now it is certain that the science has agreed to the Darwin's theory of evolution. So we are all from amoebae and so on and so forth. Everyone can attain the best given enough time and births and rebirths. Life is one of evolution and not revolution.

Metabolically it is the carbon that plays a vital role in the creation of life processes. Carbon can stably bond with four atoms and this makes it a versatile atom and is the starting point for trillions of metabolic processes. It has the ability to innovate in innumerable ways. This enables the carbon to be linked to the earth's chemistry. Metabolism is the chemical processes that maintain life. The life involves the chemical processes in the trillions of cells the body is made off.

The DNA is the ultimate measure of a living organism. There has been a avalanche of information and research on DNA soft ware. The DNA has been mapped to the last chromosomes which establish the life and its traits. They have been coded and decoded and is called the divine finger print. So far only the god knew the DNA soft ware and is now available to the scientists in the laboratory.

If the entire DNA in just one of your cells was unpacked and stretched out straight, it would be two yards long. Since you have about five trillion (5,000,000,000,000) cells in your body, the total length of DNA packed into you would stretch from here to the sun and back 30 times! (Science today)

To grasp the amount of DNA information in one cell, "a live reading of that code at a rate of three letters per second would take thirty-one years, even if reading continued day and night.. It has been determined that 99.9% of your DNA is similar to everyone's genetic makeup. So your uniqueness is embedded in that 0.1% that belongs only to you. This code identifies you and your behavior. (Science today)

On June 26, 2000, President Clinton congratulated those who completed the human genome sequencing. President Clinton said, "Today we are learning the language in which God created life. We are gaining ever more awe for the complexity, the beauty, the wonder of God's most divine and sacred gift."

Dr. Francis Collins, director of the Human Genome Project said - it is humbling for me and awe inspiring to realize that we have caught the first glimpse of our own instruction manual, previously known only to God."God is not only the Author of our existence, but also lays down the rules of the game of life so that existence becomes meaningful.

The nitrogen in our DNA, the calcium in our teeth, the iron in our blood, the carbon in our apple pies Prove the existence of god. Genetic code is a divine writing.- Dr. Francis Collins,

This means that all living organisms must breathe, drink, eat, and expel waste. Diet is a misunderstood term. Diet is the selection of Food and drink that leads to satiety, health, and longevity. Dieting is food deprivation, hunger, and weight control. How do we select the proper Food and drink? One should always eat with heart in mind.

Isn't there more to life than to say, Eat, drink, and be merry for tomorrow we die! Why am I here? There is more to just living and dying. Why has god created man in his own image or a woman in her own image? I am convinced that God does not play dice said Albert Einstein.

If god has written the script of life why there are so many inconsistencies? Why is there is so much of suffering? Is god not kind and merciful? What is the purpose of life? What has god ordained? If he has written what is right and wrong why we are given a choice to choose? You are not an accident, although your parents may not have planned you, but God did. Your parents are not your choice. God chose them for you.

Only God knows the plans he has for you – not the astrologer. If God is real, he created the entire universe, designed every detail, He has been, He is here, and don't you think he knows what is best for you? And He loves you, because he is love. He does not need you but you do.(VEDA). If he is love why the tyranny of sufferings, earthquakes, Tsunamis, floods, disasters, have any answers!

No matter who you are, I don't think anyone is born knowing the reason why you're here. Yes there are many instances where in the individuals are born with a purpose, seen in mythological scriptures. Rama to kill Ravana,Karthikeya to kill Tharakasura, Chamundeswari to kill Mahishasura. Krishna to restore Dharma whenever there is Adharma ruling the roost etc.

May be the reason for your birth on earth is something you will get to know on the way to your destination, the end of life. It is possible that you may not know at all! You may realize that you have not achieved what you were born for. But no one has returned to tell the tale.

The scriptures say that your current birth depends on your past. Is there an escape? Yes, build a spiritual buffer to break the cycle of births and rebirths; you are here to enrich the world. Don't go around saying the world owes you something. The world owes you nothing. It was here first.

Why am I here on earth? Where did I come from? What am I worth? Do I have any intrinsic value? These are questions you ask yourself when something untoward happens. You ask yourself in despair. When life just goes wrong you wonder why I am here. What have i done? And how can life change?

To think of it who is great? Einstein, Newton, Faraday, or CV Raman! My answer would be all of them are great in their own field. Being the richest man in the cemetery doesn't matter to me, Steve Jobs said. Steve was and still is rated as a superlative business mind.

Take a look at your own life. How would you describe it? Contented, Rushed, Exciting, Stressful, moving forward, holding back? For many of us it's all of the above at times. There are things we dream of doing one day, and there are things we wish we could forget.

The time we have on earth is few decades. It cannot be compared or measured against eternity. It is a drop in the ocean, or the equivalent of a blink of an eye. Majority of us think that we do not have in us what it makes a difference to the events on earth. Only great people can do a difference. Who is great anyway?May be the greatness is measured by the difference theymake!

The truth is, every one of us is put in this world to contribute and make a difference to the world in our own unique way. It need not be anything out of the world. It just needs to be something you do with the intention of 'doing good'. But mere intentions are what many of us have. Only a few put their intentions to work.

Nobody need wait a single moment before starting to contribute meaningfully. Your Contribution is never too small. Nobody can do everything, but everyone can do something. We live thinking that we are born only to enjoy! The difficulties, the hurt the suffering are strange and there should not be trace of them in our life. Blame god if it happens. At least are we answerable to god. Is god answerable to us, or to anyone?

As Success is not final, failure should not be fatal: One huge mistake people make in their lives is sheltering them from pain, hiding from the truth and denying reality. Be at peace with that. Violence and torture occurs, and Diseases happen. Accept it. Once you face the facts that life isn't all rainbows and butterflies, you will be more prepared to handle tough situations, and you won't take disappointment as such a shock.

As the cliché' goes, hope for the best, anticipate the worst. Be prepared! The formula for happiness is expectations divided by reality! Smile as often as possible. When you don't even feel like it. Just do it all the time. It will eventually rub off. Realize that it's okay to make mistakes. Just make sure to learn from your past mistakes, forgive yourself and move on.

When you suffer, suffer! Life isn't all about fun and games. Suffering is an inevitable part of life. We lose our jobs. We lose our loved ones. We get physically injured or sick. A loved one becomes sick. A parent dies. Learn to feel the pain intensely, and really grieve. This is a part of life, really feel the pain. And when you're done, move on, and find joy.

Human beings can't live alone. No man is a piece of stone.. No man is an island. To live consciously and courageously, to resonate with love and compassion, to awaken the great spirits within others, and to leave this world in peace, to care deeply, connect playfully, love intensely, and share generously. Try to- joyfully explore, learn, grow, and prosper. Live creatively, brilliantly, and honourably serve for the highest good of all.

The purpose of life is not merely to be happy. It is to be useful, to be honorable, to be compassionate and to make some difference that you have lived and lived well. Discovering your purpose is the easy part. The hard part is keeping it with you on a daily basis and working on yourself to the point where you become that purpose .If you don't step forward, you stand in the same place.

People who bite the hand that feeds them lick the boot that kicks them. Things will never be perfect in life. Better not to expect perfection. I am not perfect; I will never be, and I don't expect that even with all its pain, disappointment, despair and regret, I still find life interesting and meaningful. There are times when you are wounded. Out of these wounds, come new thoughts and new possibilities. Joy increases to the extent that the capacity for woe does also. Everyone wants to live on top of the mountain, but all the happiness and growth occurs while you're climbing it.

To live means to suffer, because the human nature is not perfect and neither is the world we live in. During our lifetime, we inevitably have to endure physical suffering such as pain, sickness, injury, tiredness, old age, and eventually death; and we have to endure psychological suffering like sadness, fear, frustration, disappointment, and depression. Although there are different degrees of suffering and there are also positive experiences in life that we perceive as the opposite of suffering, such as ease, comfort and happiness. Life in its totality is imperfect and incomplete, because our world is subject to impermanence.

Suffer, learn, and grow. I have suffered a lot and I am still suffering now, but I suffer calmly, with dignity, with serenity. I take suffering as part of life, a very important part. How can I learn anything if I don't suffer? But I stay calm when I suffer. Who would believe that I have deep suffering? I don't think that there should be no suffering; I don't think that there is something wrong because there is suffering; I don't think I should try to remove suffering; I do not try to overcome suffering, but I try to make suffering meaningful; I try to understand suffering deeply. No resistance. I am not depressed, agitated. I only hope that I am wise enough to understand suffering and life.

I have been bruised and battered, and bent but never broken I have not given in to suffering. I have stood my ground even in despair. No, i do not get into self indulgence. I am aware that fear of suffering is a strong emotional force that would deter you from pursuing what has caused suffering once! Heart never suffers because you are dreaming. You should face the suffering head on and not sulk or give in. Then you come out stronger and better!

Pain is subjective and is what you are made to suffer. Pain inflicts suffering. Learn the art of enjoying pain. Then you are rid of suffering. You are the master of your life. You would inculcate patience, faith and humility! Endure what is to be endured! It purifies your character and expands your soul. It makes you a better soul. Every trial makes you strong and every tribulation wiser!

All the things that happened to me in the past brought me here. Since I'm living a meaningful and peaceful life in the present moment now, the past with all the trials and tribulations is fine with me. I forgive myself and everybody responsible for it, and I am grateful to all of them for what they have done to me or for me.

Forgiving others for my suffering! Can I forgive others for my mistakes? My sufferings- are they entirely because of my mistakes only! Others connected with it are not responsible? Is it not out of place to forgive them? Yes, i feel lonely! I feel terrible! Forgive myself for the mistakes not committed by me! Well all is well in love and war! Who am I is in war with?

Mere telling others even repeatedly does not convey the gravity of your pain- both physical and Meta physical! Only the person who has undergone such a pain may be able to gauge the intensity and certainly not others. Moreover it may be better not to tell others about your suffering because firstly they may not be bothered and secondly they are able to offer you only lip sympathy. Worse some mat take vicarious pleasure that it happened to you.

. Many of us turn to god and ask him "Why me"? What have i done to you? We may even recount all the so called offerings made to the god. Some even threaten him that they will take shelter in some other god. They go to the extent of telling him

"You do not understand my agony". Finally they end up saying that he has no clue whatsoever of their suffering. God seems to say "Yes i have no clue either"

Agree to disagree and to accept the inevitable are the greatest virtues any one can have. Your mind is is at peace. Life has to be lived forwards. There are so many virtues to be inculcated and as many vices to get rid off as age! Accept the conflicts that are inevitable. Always keep those points where there is no agreement to the last. Close in on agreeable points; finally solve the conflicts with dialogue and give and take.

Without conflicts life will be monotonous, we lose our ability to hear new ideas and work together toward creative solutions. Be innovative. Accept the challenges .encourage a healthy dissent and you will grow in stature! The suppression of conflict, on the other hand, leads to stagnation and conformity. To be in conflict with people is tiring. Yes i agree. But also remember that all conflicts need not be addressed!

The problem is not the problem.

The possibilities for miscommunication are endless, leading to conflicts. The site of this battle, Sigmund Freud tells us, is the ego, the place where our inner selves meet the external world. Every person seeks a balance between their internal state and their relation to reality. But when our self-image comes into conflict with reality, our ego-identity is called into question. This is intrapersonal conflict. Interpersonal and intergroup conflict follows as a result.

Most conflicts begin with a sense of chaos and uncomfortable feelings of fear, hurt and anger. It quickly devolves into a competitive stage where people attempt to identify who or what the problem is and establish their own position: "I am right and you are wrong." Unless this destructive pattern is circumvented and transformed into a constructive one, the conflict continues in a win/lose style. People take sides and close ranks.

People become more and more judgmental and perceptual, distortions become greater and greater. Differences are highlighted, similarities overlooked, and the desire to understand the other position deteriorates quickly. The pressure finally is not to be objective or innovative, or seek the best solution, but to win at any cost. So a temporary winner emerges, but the disagreement is really not resolved. And the subjugation of differences lays the groundwork for future internal strife. When events trigger another conflict, all the feelings and agendas from previously unresolved conflicts rise to the surface and come into play.

One of the first things to do is to draw up a contract of fair fighting -- a list of ground rules, so to speak. At base, this contract must provide for:- an attitude of mutual respect, a commitment to active listening to others, a clear focus on the participants' interdependence and mutual interests. Depending on the situation develop a - no blaming, and no personalizing of issues- speak for yourself, not for others policy to resolve the conflict.

Are you tired of living with feelings of suffering? Are you being overwhelmed and helpless? You may have martyr syndrome. Martyr syndrome is a term that describes people who use self-sacrifice and suffering to control or manipulate the events.

Stop trying to be perfect. Rather, aspire to be better than you were yesterday. Nobody is perfect. It's okay to make mistakes. Correct the mistake and move on. When you take action and face challenges, you increase your self-esteem and grow in confidence that you can handle the consequences of challenges and of change.

It is your choice whether to focus your attention on your sacrifices or to focus it on positive outcomes.

Why are we always in conflict with each other? What is the reason for this conflict? Children are in conflict with parents, Husbands are in conflict with wives, Parents are in conflict with each other. People of one religion are in conflict with people of another religion. People are at times in conflict with things or people they are not even directly connected with. It happens because we love to identify ourselves with those in conflict and feel important .There are two types of conflicts. One with people we interact with in daily life and other with people at large. Conflicts happen because our hearts are at war.

Teenagers are often in conflict with the parents because they feel that the parents are out of tune with time and stuck up in their old ways. They find the parents overbearing and dictating while parents feel that the present generation no longer respect them or listen to them. In the Internet age, where any information is just a click away, teenagers feel empowered and tend to listen to the peers more than the parents. Here again the conflict is magnified because parents feel that the sons and daughters must listen to them or learn from their experience while teenagers feel that parents do not understand their need to move with the changing times.

In case of both the parents working, at times their children feel neglected and become rebellious. Parents think that they are working hard to make the life of their 'children' comfortable and give them all the comforts which they themselves didn't get in their time, where as the children think that the parents are only concerned about their career and money but do not understand that they need their attention and love which cannot be compensated with gifts and comforts. Who is at fault? I feel both are wrong yet both are right because both are emotional and self-cantered beings. Each is only thinking about the self and looking for justification.

What is the solution to such conflicts? We have to make our hearts peaceful.

1. First of all we must feel the need to rebuild a relationship. If we want to live in peace and have love around us, we must work at all relationships. When we genuinely seek to build a relationship, we do find a way.
2. We must recognize what is wrong. We cannot look for a solution without knowing the problem.
3. Stop feeling guilty or faulted,. When we feel faulted, we find justification for our irrational behavior. Then it is difficult to see the problem.
4. Stop trying to change others or make them see your point of view without seeing their point of view.
5. Learn to see things from the other people's perspective.
6. Change yourself before changing others.
7. We must learn to communicate and speak out our thoughts clearly and seek other person's response with a peaceful mind.
8. Our tone and mannerism affect the passage of communication. We must be polite and civil with each other.
9. We must listen to other person with an open mind because only then we can truly grasp the feelings of the other person.

One cannot force one's own thoughts on others. One cannot say that I am right and all others are wrong. We must have our heart at peace and have genuine love for fellow beings to find the solution to any conflict. We have to stop treating people as objects. We must understand that all hearts seek love and feel the hurt. Treat others with love and understanding. Caring heart never finds faults with others but finds solution to dissolve the differences.

To desire for the esteem, appreciation, and regard of people is like wanting to be on a pedestal.. Be kind to people but don't try to please them. Don't be an angel. It is hard enough to be a decent human being. Being too good might mean ending up being too bitter.

Love yourself, Love thy neighbour.`

It always happens! Yes I love myself, a lot. I love my neighbour and more so his wife! The god has ordained. This love thy neighbour concept is only limited to seeking pleasures. I owe no duty. I owe no responsibility. God has not ordained that! How disgusting!

It is the paradox of life. We think we're important. That is a delusion. We see what we want to see. We see what we are shown! We are not going to see what the truth is. We do not seek truth. Yes often the truth is not palatable or pleasant!

Do what we can without expecting that people will remember what we have done for them. We want to be important in other people's lives. It is a mirage. It is a measure of the self importance we attach to ourselves. We want to feel and believe that we make a big difference in other people's lives. You try too hard to be kind to people only for self propagation. Desires, obsessions and possessions possess you. Free yourself from your impulses.

Not believing that you have a purpose won't prevent you from discovering it, just as a lack of knowledge of gravity won't prevent you from tripping or prevent an apple falling from the tree.

Trust, even when your heart begs you not to. Frolic, even when you are made fun of. Never ever be afraid of sleeping thinking what the dreams might bring. Run, even when it feels like you can't any more. Because the pain of all your experience is what makes you the person you are now. And without your experience, you are an empty page, a blank notebook, a missing lyric. What makes you brave is your willingness to live through your life and hold your head up high. So don't live life in fear.

Midlife crisis happens to everyone. The children move away. Loss of parents and some near and dear ones can be devastating. You have reached a professional road block; competition with the talented young can be difficult if not impossible. Your declining health can be a serious issue particularly if you are not backed up with insurance. You may not be able to be independent. Your mobility may be restricted. These issues are scary at times but one has to face the reality.

Balancing these issues is highly critical. Grow old gracefully. In order to achieve this you should plan to get old gracefully. Do your exercises regularly, take adequate medical care, plan your finances. Insure yourself adequately- I am very grateful to life. It has taught me so much. I want to live a long life so that I can learn more and give more.

I believe that variety is the spice of life. Lead a simple life and you will be wealthy. You will always have something for your need and not for your greed. I feel that one cannot stop progress. Your reach should be higher than your grasp.

Time tide waits for none. Time passes. So does tide! You may be feeling lonely. Your feelings for others may change and so does the others feelings for you. There are conflicts to be resolved. You are getting old and you may have fading memories. Everything goes in circles. What has gone down to the bottom will have to come up to the top. It is not out of context to mention that there could be some square pegs in round holes or is it round pegs in square holes.

Life is full of paradoxes. Good memories denote happiness but it can make you cry. The relations who are forever may not last forever. Friends whom you have helped will just let you down when you are down. They just leave you and go as if you never existed. When you need them they are never around. Forgive and forget. Even better forgive and may not forget. Never ever get stumped by them again in your life.

I really wonder why people suddenly change after they get what they wanted from you That One day you are important to them, the next day you are nothing., They serve lies wrapped in ribbons & the worst part is that kind of people still get what they want in life and we are left behind crying because them. That is life. Why should we follow all the rules of the game only to be kicked around! Just forget. It can be sickening.

My religion

This is my simple religion. There is no need for temples, no need for complex philosophy of life. The heart and your mind together make the temple. Let Kindness be your hymns to pray. Stand on your feet firmly on the ground and look up to the sky for challenges. Be compromising in conflict and when you govern do not control.

Believe that work is worship and enjoy what you do. Truth is always simple. Half truths are white lies. I never separate the life I lead from the words I speak.

In life do not manipulate. Keep the life Simple. That's how life is lived. Tell the truth. It's a good policy to cover your nakedness. it's a good policy to be able to be modest. Follow ethics and live ethically and refrain from engaging in bad deeds.. I love success. But successes are few and far between. Life is long and slow. But it's life. Being positive about it just improves the likelihood that it will work, and it makes it more pleasant too. There is only one expert I can trust with my health. That is me.

If Heart has a soul, Brain has Mind!

Biology gives you a brain. Life turns it into a mind- Heart is soulful. Brain is mindful-

Heart supplies blood to the brain and supplies oxygen to it. Brain and as matter fact all organs in the body need oxygen for survival and be able to perform their functions adequately. If the heart does not perform adequately all organs in the body become dysfunctional. If the blood pressure generated by the heart is less than 60mm of mercury due to say a myocardial infarction the first organ that becomes dysfunctional would be the brain.

Brain has no capacity to function in an anoxic or Hypoxic state. Brain death occurs if the blood pressure and the blood supply are not restored within four to five minutes. Even though the heart has recovered and started functioning normally after 5 minutes the brain cannot regain its function. The heart can function normally for two to three weeks even after brain death occurs as seen in many road accidents.

The heart can be transplanted to a person with an irrecoverable heart disease. That is the beauty of the heart, Now please decide as to who is stronger Brain or Heart. They cannot exist without the other. One depends on the other for optimal functions. If it is true that there are as many minds as there are heads but when the heart speaks, the mind finds it indecent to object.

The brain has to evolve to have an evolved mind. If it does not it is as good as a snake which cannot cast its skin off. We have a tendency to lose connection with the heart in favour of the Brain and through it to mind. Our modern society encourages this, which compounds the problem.

Mind is a non-physical or non physiological phenomenon. Mind has no anatomical limitations or boundaries. Mind has to perceive something and you are there! Mind functions at two levels- One ar the conscious level and the other at a subconscious level. The function at the conscious level is worldly and is aware of the environment with both fight and Flight response. Is mind the seat of knowledge? The brain is the physical entity that has the centres for memory, knowledge, for speech, cognition vision etc. Sky is the limit for the mind with no barriers or anatomic limitations.

Mind is, or can function like a mirror and can reflect you to yourself. it is estimated that only 20% of the brain in its physical form is used in the day to day life by the ordinary and general population. Rest of the Brain is dormant. Anybody who can even use 10% of this dormant form in addition to the 20% he will be the most brilliant. We know less; think less, experience less, imagine less. So we are less than what we are. We always seem to talk more.

Change is inevitable; growth is optional-

It happens whether we are ready or not.

Change is inevitable. Nothing stays still. Life is in constant motion from the molecular to the planetary level. The universe moves in harmony with the cosmic. rhythm. Then why is change the source of so much fear and unhappiness? faced with the inevitable changes of life, what can we do? We can learn the arts of adaptation, self-preservation and creative living. Change isn't something we have to suffer.

Explore the forces of change, discover the benefits of change. Change is inevitable

On that we all agree. However, it just may not be the change that you imagine.

I would like to think I am mature, Does it make me mature just because, by definition, I am an adult? There is an ambiguous line that separates being young with being old. I think, more than anything, maturity means being okay with change. It's about acknowledging that change will happen, and it's out of our control.

Change often feels hard because it puts us outside of what is familiar – our habitual patterns of thinking and behaving. Change is a direct affront to our comfort zone.

Accept the things to which fate binds you, and love the people with whom fate brings you together, but do so with all your heart. There is no need for temples; no need for complicated philosophy, our own brain, our own heart is our temple. Your time is limited, so don't waste it living someone else's life. Don't be trapped by dogma - which is living with the results of other people's thinking. Don't let the noise of others' opinions drown your own voice, and most important, have the courage to follow your heart and intuition. The heart has its reasons which reason does not understand.

Heart attack is when the blood flow to the heart is restricted causing the heart cells to die. Panic attack is a condition where a person experiences a sudden onset of fear, nervousness and/ or apprehension. It is known as a panic disorder and is a serious condition. Panic disorders strike without reason, without warning and can last somewhere between minutes to hours.

Heart attack and panic attack are two different conditions that a person can suffer from. These both conditions are often confused as they may share similar symptoms. Both can with the other and independently as well and can make matters worse. In all consideration, these are two different conditions. Heart attack can result in a person dying, while panic will cause fainting at the most. Heart attack deals with the heart, while panic deals with the mind.

No one wants to die. Even people who want to go to heaven don't want to die to get there, and yet death is the destination we all share. No one has ever escaped it. That is as it should be because- it is the Execution of Life- clears out the old to make way for the new-

Gratitude unlocks the fullness of life. It turns what we have into enough, and more. It turns denial into acceptance, chaos to order, confusion to clarity. It can turn a meal into a feast, a house into a home, a stranger into a friend.

When you have a conflict, is heart at fault? Is heart responsible for all the feelings and emotions? Is Mind at fault as the feelings and emotions are triggered by the mind in the brain!

It's okay to follow your heart but take your brain with you.

A man says a lot of things in summer he doesn't mean in winter. What is said in the night may not mean anything in the morning! As i have said before the heart has its reasons which mind knows not. Does the mind represent a cold neurotic behaviour or is it the work of the brain which has centres for different emotions. Is Mind a conduit for the soul? Does the soul inspire the heart? The sounds of the heart go unheard and the soul has departed from the body.

The heart has no pain receptors! So the next time someone breaks your heart just move on! Your pain is just an illusion, a temporary psychological disturbance that you have to overcome. . In short, it's all in the mind. This conscious mind does all the logical and rational thinking. It is that which invented the wheel also invented the fire. Obviously, we humans give a lot of value to it since it had made our life so much easier. Unfortunately, the mind does not make decision-making easier for us. Well, sometimes, yes.

It is the mind that makes the comparisons, reasons the rationale on the pros and cons of the choices and comes up with a solution that is often practical with respect to the mind's own projection of the future consequences. The mind often uses the past experiences and its imaginative projection of the future as reference points to come up with a choice that is best for the now.

One has to remember that such derivations based on past and future need not necessarily be right. There is a school of thought which propounds that- NOW is all that there is, everything else past and future, does not exist.

When life gives you a hundred reasons to cry, show life that you have a thousand reasons to smile! Emotional reasoning, which prevails in matters of the heart, is different from intellectual reasoning. Are these two types of reasoning condemned to fight each other, or can they be integrated?

"The head or the brain is always fooled by the heart,"-why on earth the heart should bother to fool the head. A rational person knows that under certain conditions it is better to follow emotional tendencies than to use more elaborate intellectual processes.

The issue is complex. Is love rational? Why always one falls in love and not rise in love! The conflicts between the mind and heart are articulated in immeasurable ways in day to day life. One should listen to the heart beats. When it is silent listen to the mind. As I have said before it's okay to follow your heart but take your brain with you.

If we know how to create a symbiosis between the two systems, we will have the best of both worlds. Love is in the mind, not in the heart, or is it in the Brain? Love – what is it? Brain imaging studies are allowing scientists to give at least a partial answer. Passion is deeply associated with the heart; love will in fact be in the mind. A recent study shows love is a complex emotion triggered by 12 specific areas of the brain — the network of love.

What is the major difference between the Heart and the mind, especially in functional terms? The heart is a muscular pump and a spectacular one at that. There is nothing spiritual about the heart. It may beat faster when you're aroused or afraid, but that is just an involuntary reaction driven by your central nervous system.

The mind, then, could be seen as the functionality of a brain .

The mind is where we calculate how to receive pleasure, where we make decisions between what is right and wrong and how we live our lives. It is our "self", our conscience. The heart is an organ; it keeps us alive and so is essential to us. It is also the organ that governs our feelings. This is in fact false, because we do it with our brain, but there is no denying the fact that it is an important symbol of life, emotions and tradition.

Logical, rational thinking is attributed to the brain or the mind of a person, but when it comes to emotional thinking, it is the heart that takes precedence over his mind. When we think about feelings or emotions, we make use of our heart, or so to speak. Of course, we do know that mind -brain and the heart are just two different organs inside our body, but their differences are not limited to their looks and functions, but how we perceive or look at these differences. I try to differentiate between hearts and mind not on the basis of physics but on the basis of thinking of human beings.

Heart of the mind is soul or Mind of the heart is soul! If, Mind is attributed to the Brain, Does the soul belong to the heart?

I am a professional Cardiac surgeon. I have operated on thousands of hearts! I have seen and felt every nook and corner of the heart while performing open heart surgery. I have operated on a child's heart, a parent's heart, a lover's heart and hearts of all categories. I have sought to see a child in the parents heart, lover in lovers heart, A wife in a husbands heart and a husband in a wife's heart. I want to put it on record that I have not seen anyone in anyone's heart. So do not blame the heart for any failure of love in all its forms.

Heart governs our mind when we are in love while, in all other life situations, it is the mind that takes precedence over heart.

Heart facts

Your heart beats about 100,000 times in one day and about 35 million times in a year. During an average lifetime, the human heart will beat more than 2.5 billion times.

Your body has about 5.6 litres of blood. These 5.6 litters of blood circulate through the body three times every minute. In one day, the blood travels a total of 19,000 km (12,000 miles)

Though the heart weighs only 11 ounces on average, a healthy heart pumps 2,000 gallons of blood through 60,000 miles of blood vessels

The heart is the hardest working muscle in the body. Every day, it creates enough energy to drive a lorry over 30 kilometres. Over a lifetime, that's equivalent to driving to the moon and back each day.

During an average lifetime, the heart will pump nearly 1.5 million barrels of blood. A pumping human heart can squirt blood 9.1 metres. If your arteries, veins and capillaries were laid out end to end they would measure 100,000 km. That's nearly enough to stretch two and a half times around the planet! (Astounding facts about the human body)

Women's heart beats faster than that of men. Depression is an illness that affects many levels of health. We tend to think first of the drastic changes in mood and vitality: hopelessness, lost energy, confused thinking, broken self-esteem, paralysis of will - and thoughts of ending life.

It is natural for anyone to fall in love with what one loves- More so, if this love is romantically involved. Both have to love each other. If the love is one sided it is like a shadow boxing or punching in the air. To fall in love is awfully simple, but to get out of love is simply awful-

Every man has his secret sorrows.

Think positive and stay healthy and normal. Be happy for what you have and what you are and cherish it. Remove the word 'I' from your vocabulary and you will find happiness.

If you are husband to a wife the duties that husbands have to women are many. There are many enforcement agencies and councils that the society has created. These can be quiet forcible and enforceable in a heavy handed manner. A husband has to love his wife, his own wife and not someone else's! It is the inherent weakness of men as husbands to love other's wives.

The men as husbands are given no option. I remember an incident i read long back. A man inserts an advertisement in the news papers 'Want a wife'. Within half an hour he got five hundred telegrams/ mails 'Take Mine', a mirror for the popularity of Wives. Often, what goes under the name of love has little to do with love. The word 'love' has become a word to describe the wants of the body. You are required to love her in sickness and in health, for better or for worse, for richer or poorer? All this for life and beyond!

Can love be codified? If yes is love a Contract? Is it a Duty? What are these live in relationships? Everything is shared from home to finances to children to fathering and everything! Love is divine! Who says that after seeing all this?

When love is reduced to contracts, duties and for a time may be all these are pre requisites. Where the warmth and affection have gone, may be in search of love. There are only regulations and conditions and pre requisites. There is no love.

The first duty of love is to listen. I read this today and am struck by the simplicity. And yet, many of us might agree that even in its simplicity, it is a rare thing today-To listen. Listen to your wife and give her quality time and the love sprouts again.

A duty does not entail anything in return. Deal is between equals and there is something in return on agreed terms. Is love a deal?- A contract between a man and a woman.

In the society as it exists now the relationships in marriage between men and women are not on equal terms, on the man's side we have duties and obligations, along with a very heavy dose of accountability and responsibility, while on the woman's side, we have rights and options, without the burden of much of accountability. In situations of conflicts wife has the benefit of doubt.

The wife has rights and more rights. She has many enforcing agencies at her service which are merciless and can be high handed in favor of wife. In Dowry harassment act the husband is first arrested and then the enquiry begins. It is one of the most misused acts in India.

A successful man is one who makes more money than his wife can spend. I remember, Socrates saying- A successful woman is one who can find such a man. This tells the complete story of Man, woman, love lust and marriage.

When a man opens a car door for his wife, it's either a new car or a new wife.

A good wife always knows her place. Behind every successful man is a woman, behind her is his wife. Behind every unsuccessful man there are many. A wife should be an indispensable part of the husband.. God expects you to help your man;

Admittedly, men are not complete. God was not satisfied when he made Adam. So he developed a master piece Eve overcoming the deficiencies in Adam. The worst thing a man can do is to marry the wrong woman. Blessed are the hearts that can bend but never be broken. You know what charm is a way of getting the answer 'yes' without having asked any question.

Sorrow

Is absence of happiness a state of sorrow?if you are hapy all the time you do not need god. God sees to that the durations of happiness is always bordered with events that makes you sad or sorrow. God is scared that you will forget him.Now who needs whom? Both need the other.

It is said that sorrows make you tolerant, kind and understanding, it makes you more human. It keeps you humble. Happiness if the state persists all the time makes you uncaring, intolerant and wicked and punishing. Nothing succeeds like success. God keeps you going.

Trust the one who could see three things in you, sorrow behind your smile, and love behind your anger and meaning behind your silence.

We are always worried about something or the other. The worry turns into fear. Fear of tomorrow, fear of what happened yesterday and its possible advent in future, fear of pain, of hunger, of illness, of finances and finally of fear of passing away.

A pregnant mom is afraid of delivery and the pain. She would want the pregnancy to proceed to the term. She is worried about the child. She is frightened about a possible damage to the health of the child and so on. When you are born the world around will smile and be happy only when they hear you cry. Live a life that when you die the world is crying wanting more of you. Never do anything that the world gives a sigh of relief that you have indeed died at last.

The hurt and its memory of suffering even long back will not fade. The event may have passed off but the memory of the event and the hurt, suffering lasts may be forever.

This sense of hurt and the suffering can have a life changing consequence if taken positively. The memory will not allow the event to be repeated. You would be equipped with dealing with the situation. May be it even makes you more human!

Sorrows in life are inevitable. It May be an act of god to tame you. Let not the journey of life be overshadowed by the sufferings. Do not make the sorrow inconsolable. Let not the intensity of the sorrow paralyze you into inactivity. Weep and cry and then get on with the job. Do not die many deaths before you die because of the sorrow.

Sorrows soften the heart and mellows you, tames you for the good. Do not brood over the loss. Have faith and move on in life. Let not the sorrows and the hurts eclipse the sunshine out of your life. Do not shut yourself in mindprison. The world is a large landscape for you to paint greener events of your life.

Time heals. Really!

Time heals! Time does not bring relief; you all have lied who told me time would ease my pain-

Yes in some instances which are not serious or small hurts- by the wonderful gift of god- The art of forgetting!

Healthy remembrance may not be bad after all. It has a positive spin off on your system. One will be equipped to deal with such situations in life. The lingering memory will help coordinate your strategies much better than before. Learn to stare the sorrow in the face and believe me the effect gets down sized considerably.

As a man you are not expected to cry. But still you cry, weep and be done with it and get on with your life. Remember the trials and tribulations will make you strong. The hurt will soften your rough edges and makes you more human. Show courage in the face of sorrows and hurts. Be patient. Laughing faces do not mean that there is absence of sorrow. But it means that they have the ability to deal with it.

The world has been created in such a way that stronger thrives on the weak. Each species is born with ability to sustain to some extent but are not beyond the reach of the stronger. The speed of the deer, colours of the snakes, poison of their bites, the shape and girth of some animals help them ward of the stronger species etc.

If we look around in the natural world, countless myriads of diverse life forms are all moved by the instinct of self-preservation.

They seek only such conditions as would give them sustenance, pleasure, comfort, and avoid those that endanger their lives.

Anxiety is when you can't stop the fear of your own thoughts; Feel trapped in your body like a prisonerand not knowing when this will all end is the worst of all. . In many ways, I have a reasonably good life. Nevertheless, a part of me will always be sad as long as there is suffering in this world. Life is bitter sweet. And that's OK with me. Happiness without sadness would not be complete…as long as suffering persists. I sat with the feelings of sadness, gazing at the dark night sky. I didn't try to push them away. Quite the contrary, I felt empowered by them.

Biological life.

What is biology? Simply put, it is the study of life -- life in all of its grandeur. From the very small algae to the very large elephant, life has a certain wonder about it. With that in mind, how do we know if something is living? Is a virus alive or dead? What are the characteristics of life? These are all very important questions with equally important answers.

On a basic level, we can say that life is ordered. Organisms have an enormously complex organization. We're all familiar with the intricate systems of the basic unit of life, the cell. Life grows and develops and differentiates. This means more than just getting larger in size. Living organisms also have the ability to rebuild and repair themselves when injured. Life can reproduce. Life can only come from other living creatures.

People often use the phrase; I am only human, as an excuse for making mistakes. To understand what it means to be human, let us start with defining what constitutes human life. Science defines life as the possession of self-sustaining biological processes. This definition distinguishes the living from the dead.

A single cell is alive. A cell is human if the genetic blueprint of the cell is human DNA. Techniques of cellular biology make it possible to take cells from human organs and grow them in laboratory. The cells are alive and the cells are human. Life is based on DNA software. We're a DNA software system, you change the DNA software, and you change the species. It's remarkably simple in concept, remarkably complex in its execution.

All living cells that we know of on this planet are DNA software driven biological machines comprised of hundreds to thousands of protein robots coded for by the DNA software. The protein robots carry out precise biochemical functions developed by billions of years of evolutionary software changes.

We can go from the digital code to the genetic code, and now modelling the entire function of the cell in a computer, going the complete digital circle. We are going even further now, by using computer software to design new DNA software to create a new synthetic life.

Is there an intrinsic reason for it? Can we trace back this state of affairs to some kind of first principle, in order to ascertain and to understand why nothing else is compatible with the very laws of Nature? I view that we're now in what I'm calling "The Digital Age of Biology". Life is a process of dynamic renewal. We're all shedding about 500 million skin cells every day. That is the dust that accumulates in your home; that's you. You shed your entire outer layer of skin every two to four weeks. You have blood cells that die every day. If you're not constantly synthesizing new cells, you die.

Put your heart, mind and soul into even your smallest acts. This is the secret of success. Overall, what is happening on Earth is that matter is becoming ordered into larger wholes. So the theme or meaning or purpose of life is the ordering or integration or, a process that is driven by the physical law of Negative Entropy. 'Holism', which the dictionary defines as 'the tendency in nature to form wholes' and 'teleology', which is defined as 'the belief that purpose and design are a part of nature', are both terms that recognise this 'tendency' towards integration.

Self Perfect or Imperfect!

I am imperfect, but I try and lead a more engaged life today – Live simple and not simply live, Lead with Spirit Always try to do the right things right and Take time to reboot the soul. Interestingly, the bottom line of all medicine, law, religion, philosophy, and much science is the simple sentence "things aren't right" yet. Medicine tries to repair and prevent, law tries to control and correct, religion and philosophy try to explain and much of science tries to show. . Regular naps prevent old age... especially if you take them while driving.

In life we all have an unspeakable secret, an irreversible regret, an unreachable dream and an unforgettable love. The saddest summary of life contains three descriptions: could have, might have, and should have.

Why are we really here on earth? Is it all about eating, drinking and procreation! What lies behind the daily life struggles? Just as on earth we struggle to be educated, to get a job, to love and be loved, to overcome disease, to live together with others and to acquire values useful to support material life.

A child struggles to speak, to walk, to run to understand. And then death comes! So what? If death is the end of life why then are all these struggles? Or are these struggles only means to an end-An unseen end? To find the meaning of life we must look beyond this earth, to know who we are and wither our paths lead.

To understand the forces which activate life and the so called mysteries of life has given rise to different endeavors but confusion, skepticism and despair still abound. How then are we to recognize the Truth? "Spiritual bread immediately refreshes, Truth revitalizes and Light animates. I had always believed that life would happen in the future… after I had achieved 'something'. However what is that something – I am not sure even now!

When I was in school, life was something that happened in college. College did happen. And yes, it was fun. Yet, my search for life had shifted. I wanted to feel alive. I wanted to grow fast. I thought life would happen after marriage. Marriage turned out to be all those things that marriage is supposed to be-Togetherness, arguments, wonderings, hopes and all the things in between. However, after a while, I began to feel mounting dissatisfaction again. I wanted to make it big – for myself, for others… perhaps that would make me feel alive?

I became a cardiothoracic surgeon and that seemed like the perfect expression of me. With a lot of hard work and team efforts, it began to take off in a significant way. It was exciting and at times nerve-wracking. One of those evenings, after a long, tiring day when there had been one challenge after another, I sat beside my window, my chin upon my hands and in despair asked God: Where is this thing called LIFE? Why do I always seem to miss it? Where is it? Show me! I want to feel alive!

Simply selfishness is divisive or disintegrative while selflessness is integrative. So consider-others as above-yourself, altruistic, unconditional selflessness is the underlying theme of existence and the answer to the question of 'what is the meaning of life'. It's the glue that holds the world together and what we really mean by the term 'love'. If you walk continuously along a straight path, you will never be found again.

Apart from gigantic celestial bodies, it is surprising that microscopic subatomic particles inside matter like electrons are also moving in orbits around the nucleus of the atom. These are all energy particles and are responsible for matter formation and destruction.

Who am I?

That is a simple question, yet it is one without an answer. I am many things—I am a man and I am a former child and a future skeleton, and I am in a distant future a pile of dust.

I am- is a concept and thought and feeling and outfit. I am me and I am myself.. I am this and I am that. I am everything and I am nothing. I am my own worst critic. I am going to give you an example. That's not me enough. is the kind of thing I am prone to say about myself. See what I mean? I am sure you do. I am the silent majority. I am the loud minority. I am sometimes referred to as Mr Excuse Me in an annoyed tone of voice, because apparently I am in the way. I am so sorry.

Growing old is unavoidable, but growing up is optional, including refusing to grow!

The true purpose of self-reflection is to correct our mistaken thoughts and actions, and learn from them, thereby creating a more constructive life. Self-reflection is not just the simple act of discovering past mistakes and making up for these mistakes, like resetting a negative to zero. The ultimate objective of self-reflection is the development of a more positive self and the realization of a utopia on earth as the fulfillment of God's will." Sun and moon, light and night are tenets of my life's philosophy.

Disappointment's first cousin is Frustration. It takes billions of years to create a human being. And it takes only a few seconds to die. Every man has forgotten who he is. When you dissect Darwin's theory of evolution you were a amoeba, fish, frog. Various animals, monkey and finally now you are a human being.

One may understand the cosmos, but never the ego; the self is more distant than any star. I have never, in all my life, not for one moment, been tempted toward religion of any kind. The fact is that I feel no spiritual void. I have my philosophy of life.

The purpose of my life is to lead a life of purpose. I have a simple philosophy of being kind, do no harm, laugh – more often at myself! There is always someone better off than me, and there is always someone worse off. What is most important is to look at my life and know that it isn't so bad. To some people, I have everything, and to some I have nothing. To me, I have what I have and that is it!. There is no reason to stress to survive.

Scientists say the average person has roughly 70,000 thoughts each day - and is actually more active while you're sleeping. I am aware of the benefits of yoga and particularly the positive profound effects of breathing techniques practised in pranayama.

Today is today, only today. Tomorrow will be today. Tomorrow will soon be a yesterday- A yesterday can never be a today. Laziness is the habit of resting before you get tired. The energy of the mind is the essence of life. There is a larger element which has kept the universe in order.

Newton described the Newton's Laws of motion. There are three of them which govern the movements of the stars and the satellites and the universe. God is believed to have structured the universe and Newton described the laws of motion already scripted.

.

Life and Failures.

Failure is extremely difficult to handle, but those that do come out stronger. At 20 years of age- the will reigns, at 30 the wit, at 40 the judgment. I strongly believe that i have to live my own life as i i will have to die my own. You only live once, but if you do it right, once is enough. I will only walk this road once; I might as well make the most of it.

Live your life. Do not just merely exist. Just when you think it can't get any worse, it can. And just when you think it can't get any better, it does. If you don't know where you are going, any road will get you there. Never tell your problems to anyone...20% don't care and the other 80% are glad you have them. What would I do if destiny twisted the road I took? What if it threw me to a place I did not want to go? Would you fight, would run or would I accept? Set across these dilemmas I conclude 'Life is what you make of it'.

I have realized that Relationships are like birds, if you hold tightly they DIE If you hold loosely, they FLY but if you hold with care, They remain with you forever! "All this chasing -for what?" I asked myself. I treat and he Cures or may be the nature cures! Just keep the patient amused till the cure takes place!.

Anxiety, stress and Depression – are the silent killers or otherwise! It is time to wake up and change the way you live. Earn enough to meet all your needs. It's the greed that destroys you in the making of a living. We lose touch with the enormity of our inner being, and we distance ourselves from the confidence of our unique expressions.

Heaven is the place god is supposed to be living. Hell is where the god who has a check list of our worldly deeds and misdeeds resides. Can there be such a god? God is always good and pious and forgiving! Many of us do deeds that are neither good nor bad. But all our actions and deeds are recorded by one called Chithraguptha. If you have done good deeds, have spread happiness, if you have reduced the sorrow of your co passengers of journey of life then you are a candidate to go to heaven and live with god.

If you deeds are cruel, suffocating, hurting, uncaring, corrupt you go to hell.If your deeds are neither good nor bad, if you have lived life of no use to the society then you are a candidate for rebirth. Again if are to be reborn as a human being the record of some of the good deeds should be greater. If not you could be born as any of the thousands of species in the world.

Heaven is a place of everlasting reward for the righteous to go after they die. Hell in comparison is a place of eternal torment for the wicked. It is assumed that the people who are righteous and do gooders are less in number as the prerequisites are stringent. You find more people in the hell or many or in the transit back to earth.

The only thing you achieve in life without effort is failure. The Serenity Prayer: God, grant me the serenity to accept the things I cannot change, courage to change the things I can, and wisdom to know the difference. Heart may be on the left, but it is always right, When You Were Born, You Cried and the World Rejoiced, Live Your Life in a way that When You Die The World Cries And You Rejoice. I do not know if one should rejoice at one's own end. No one has come back to tell whether they rejoiced or regretted.

Prayer is when you talk to God; meditation is when you listen to God. . Medicine tries to repair and prevent, law tries to control and correct, religion and philosophy try to explain and much of science tries to show.

I ask you—Risk more than others think is safe.

I ask you—Care more than others think is wise.

I ask you—Dream more than others think is practical.

Beauty's only skin deep but ugly goes down to the bone. Remember that the praise of fools is a censure in disguise. Don't value yourself harshly in the process.

Have a small, but comfortable home, Buy less, go for quality more, and put the spare money in the savings account for a rainy day or a reward vacation. Do not jump to solve others problems. First let your life be without any problems. I urge you to learn to say NO. If you can't say no, you'll always be the person who is trying to fix everyone else's problems as well as your own.

Perish the thought that you are intelligent and do not credit yourself more importance than you deserve. You are certainly not indispensible to others. Believe me the others can solve the issues themselves. Do not mess up more. Don't try to please others by neglecting yourself. Use your instincts. Don't be easily led. If you feel there is something wrong, there probably is.

Worry is the first cousin of fear. So do not worry and be happy! Worrying and stress go hand in hand so stop worrying to avoid stress. To be your self is to take care of yourself. Do not hurt yourself, do not neglect yourself. Do not have a low self esteem. Be proud of yourself. There are always a few antacids and laxatives are there to cure the combination of managerial flatulence and organizational constipation.

Not all those who wander are lost in the journey of life. Standing still is the fastest way of moving backwards in a rapidly changing world. No man ever got high by pulling others down.

Human creation

Human creation starting as a zygote with the fusion of sperm and the ovum to a trillion cell human form is a marvel. We do not realise the greatness of the creation and limit ourselves with petty bickering and downright inhuman deeds and indulge in hurting others and in selfish deeds. And yet, amidst all of this, we find ourselves bewildered by the contradictions, conflicts, and hypocrisies that abound. Where are the solutions for a world filled with so many obvious problems of human suffering that we all have either experienced or observed—the problems of poverty, racism and oppression.

If I were to propose a way of looking at the world . . . I would single out an "ethos of symbiosis." I am talking about the kind of mentality that favours harmony over opposition, unity over division, "we" over "I." Practically, it is expressed as the idea that human beings should live in harmony with othes and with nature. We seek peace. We desire that wonderful sense of harmony and being cantered in life. We desire the calmness, tranquillity, and serenity that is the heart of peace.

Life is simple - people make it difficult

Distractions occupy the mind and take our focus away from the moment. The solution to this is to reduce distractions. Do something new. It doesn't have to be anything grand. A little change is all it takes to have a new experience.

Be careful while interacting with people who have negative fallout. Toxic people are people who have a negative influence on your life. The most dangerous toxic people in your life are the ones you haven't yet identified.

Sometimes weakness is the opposite of strength, but sometimes weakness can be the pathway to strength. Sometimes addiction is the opposite of sobriety, but sometimes addiction can be the pathway to sobriety. Sometimes infidelity is the opposite of fidelity, but sometimes infidelity can be a pathway to fidelity. Sometimes failure is the opposite of success, but sometimes failure can be the pathway to success."

Everything that happens in our life happens for a reason and sometimes that means we must face heartaches in order to experience joy.

The phrase "I'm spiritual, but not religious," is an apt description of our inner desire to connect on a spiritual plane, to find true meaning, value and fulfillment and to discover what works for me.

Religion has brought much suffering over the centuries, and for that reason many have decided to reject the idea of God altogether. However, religion and God are two separate things. Man-made religious traditions contrast greatly with. the passionate, close relationship that God desires to have with you and me. It takes courage to be different. Most people go with the flow – that's what dead fish do, or so they say! It's easy to follow the crowd, only to discover that they're going in the wrong direction.

Until you make peace with yourself, or you'll never be content with what you have. A sense of inadequacy often informs the question around "Who am I?" cosmologists trying to understand the origin of the universe, biologists working on evolution or psychologists studying behavior are driven by the same desire to know. Or perhaps I shouldn't speak for anyone else and only say that for me it is this way.

I, Me and Myself- I am indeed referring to the same person, but they are not interchangeable. Eventually I realized that "normal" was only a concept in my own mind. In fact, my "normal" wasn't the same as someone else's normal. Even my "normal "was unique. And in fact it was just a way of limiting myself, a concept rooted in fear to begin with.

Realize that you are not like anyone else on earth. No one on this planet is exactly the same as you are, even if you have a twin. It's not even close. Your individual collection of experiences makes you unique. Yet what do most people do with this uniqueness? They try to forget it. They cling to the past, thinking that one needs to be like everyone else.

They strive to be similar to everyone else. Trying to be a Roman in Rome Syndrome! This is pure folly, since similarity and normalcy doesn't exist except as an imaginary concept. Have you ever met a 100% normal person? Are you normal? Or is there anything unique about you that separate you from the pack?

"Normal" isn't a label worthy of your pursuit. It's worthless. Perhaps you're worried that if you're too different, you'll be ostracized. You will be ostracized by other fear-driven normality seekers, but their acceptance is basically worthless anyway.

Truth raises your consciousness. First, accept the truth. Whatever you're afraid to know lowers your consciousness. Secondly, speak the truth. If honesty is a challenge for you, it's because you aren't being honest enough with yourself. Lies you tell others are shadowed by lies you tell yourself.

Courage raises your consciousness. "Whatever I fear, I must face." Compassion raises your consciousness. Compassion is the root of unconditional love, a feeling of connectedness with everything that exists. Do you feel connected to yourself, to others and To animals? To all living things? To everything that exists? The more you develop this connection, the more conscious and aware you become.

Today I am, tomorrow will soon be yesterday. Do you ever regret the future before it has even happened? When you regret, fear, or worry about the future, you project your consciousness beyond the present moment. Essentially you become unconscious because you lose awareness of the present moment, and consequently, you lose awareness of the real you, which exists only in the present. Not being faultless myself, I won't presume to probe into the faults of others.

The future is something of an illusion because you never actually exist there. Past and future are merely memories and projections. Your real experiences occur only in the present.

Who has space for Emptiness? Who has time for Eternity? Who among the lonely has room for Solitude? I think heaven has the better climate, but hell has the better company- so why worry. Worrying is like a rocking chair, it gives you something to do, but it gets you nowhere.

There always seems to be plenty to worry about, and worry we do—from nagging concerns to full-blown anxiety. It's time to stop worrying and instead create a more peaceful, powerful, and purposeful life. Health is an issue everyone is worried about.

Seth Godin defines anxiety and worry as "Practicing failure in advance." And that's the most perfect description I have ever read. Successful people see failure as an acceptable risk and don't take failure personally. You can find relief from the anxiety that controls you. You Can Overcome Anxiety.

Worrying is carrying tomorrow's load with today's strength- It is moving into tomorrow ahead of time. Worrying doesn't empty tomorrow of its sorrow, it empties today of its strength. How would your life be different if...You stopped worrying about things you can't control and focus on the things you can?

Do not trouble- trouble till trouble troubles You! Look at the birds of the air; they do not sow or reap or store away in barns, and yet god feeds them. Are you not much more valuable to Him than birds? Therefore do not worry about tomorrow. Let tomorrow worry about itself. Each day has enough trouble of its own. I have known a great many troubles, but most of them have never happened. Never feel threatened or feel vulnerable. Seek solace in the company of prayer and Meditation. Prayer is when you talk to god and Meditation is when you listen to god.

38% worry every single day. Worry executes more people than work at any given time. But if you're preoccupied with "what ifs" and worst-case scenarios, worry become a problem. Unrelenting doubts and fears can be paralyzing. They can sap your emotional energy, send your anxiety levels soaring, and interfere with your daily life. It is a fact that your heart will last till you live and you live till your heart lasts. Don't worry about the world coming to an end today. It is already tomorrow in Australia.

permanence of life or its impermanence!

I've been thinking a lot about the meaning of life and the impermanent nature of it all- The impermanence of a rainbow - beautiful while it's there, and just as likely to have disappeared by the time you blink. Today you are. For tomorrow have faith. It is like taking the first step even if you don't see the staircase. Impermanence and change are thus the undeniable truths of our existence.

The child is not the same when it grows up and becomes a young man, an adult in the waiting, nor when he turns into an old man. The seed is not the tree, and the fruit is also not the tree, though it is produced by the tree. The butterfly counts not months but moments, and has time enough to make it beautiful.

Butter flies are perfect examples of harmony and purpose in life. Both wings are in perfect harmony. A butter fly with one wing is not alive. The butterflies draw our notice simple because of their beauty and selfless service of pollination. The flower carries the color which the tree did not have. The fruit carries the color and sweetness which neither the flower nor the tree had. All thanks to butter flies which cross pollinate.

As a child grows to be a teenager,, to be a youth to be an adult and Then he gets old. He may get sick and die. Body is perishable. This is the journey of life.

We know cell divisions take place in each living being continuously. Old cells in our bodies die and yield place continuously to the new ones that are forming. Surely it is better to be like a butterfly, spreading love, sharing happiness, giving life, sharing beauty, and giving lessons on how to lead a happy life. Butterflies are not insects,' their passage from flower to flower is like a Ballet in the air.

Bill Gates used the power of money to change the world, and mother Teresa used the power of love to change the world. Money is greater than love! So be it!

The end of that story is the beginning of an audacious possibility. As humanity, we have understood intellectual quotient and even emotional quotient but what the world needs now is CQ - Compassion Quotient. It is an intelligence of the heart. There are actually neurons not just in our brain but also in our heart.

The question I have is - who helped India more mother Teresa or Bill Gates?

MotherTeresa said 'Give until it hurts'. I'm not sure if Gates is feeling any pain after Melinda- Gates foundation was started! Intellectuals simply cannot connect the wealth of a Bill Gates with the creative processes as in arts and culture.

Stolen wealth..

The recent finding by Patrick French -India: A Portrait is that more than two-thirds of the under-40 members of the Look Sabha are hereditary and many of them are hyper-hereditary, based on their dynasty.

Have courage for the great sorrows in life, and patience for the small ones. Always remember-A man can be happy with any woman as long as he does not love her .Always forgive your enemies, nothing annoys them so much-The face of the enemy frightens me only when I see how much it resembles me.

If God is with us, who can be against us?

Who is God?

No, I am not. I am sure of that!

No "credit" is given to God for years, decades, or even centuries of peaceful weather. God created the whole universe and the laws of nature. Most natural disasters are a result of these laws at work at cross purposes..

Why does God allow bad things to happen to good people? OR the rules minded almighty allow good things to happen to bad people. Do you have any answer? The ways of god are frustrating!

Is god perfect? I do not know for sure! Maybe the answer is Yes and No. It shows a lack of certain trust in him. the truth is we are not in charge. In reality it is God who is in charge of all of His creation. Everything that happens is either caused by or allowed by God.

Expression of anger at god is out of frustration and a way of telling him that he has done wrong! Man has no power over the will of nature.. The earth is not immune to disasters. How do we explain the suffering that accompanies such disasters? There's no doubt about it—natural disasters aren't very good for God's kindness and his standing.. Man needs someone to rely on and to even blame someone sometimes for anything!

The Observer newspaper's memorable headline caught it well: "Our Image of God must go". He believes that we need new images of God - ones that enable us to speak of the mystery of everyday experience. I'm having a hard time understanding how humans are both born in sin and created in God's image.

People believe "God exists" and "God does not exist". If there is a default position, then it is "I don't know. Doubt is useful for a while. But we must move on. To choose doubt as a philosophy of life is akin to choosing immobility as a means of transportation.

Why did God make Man? Do you know WHY you were born? What is God's Purpose for our lives? Does our existence end with death or does God have a plan beyond the grave! From dust you are, and to dust you shall return. What next?

Man's Creation of God

I don't know if God exists, but it would be better for His glory if He didn't what with all the destructive events happening day in day out!

People from long time ago think that they have to create one as mighty powerful called GOD. Why they need to create GOD? They thought they need to create "GOD" because Humans need something to be feared for. Thus GOD was created.

The theory of Evolution created great turmoil between the religious and scientific micro-cultures. When the theory was presented by Charles Darwin to the Linnaean Society of London in 1858, many religious zealots wanted him hanged for heresy.

The emergence of the belief in the supernatural in human nature can be seen as a natural consequence of the laws governing evolution. In order for the concept of the supernatural to emanate from general scientific principles, it must be substantiated by the theory of evolution.

After millions of years of evolution, most perceive the world by their instincts. Therefore, the concept of god must have originated in conjunction with the evolution of a brain capable of perceiving it.

The chaotic, unpredictable nature of weather created a problem because they needed rain for their crops to grow. They were at the mercy of whatever force controlled the weather. And so, man could have invented the concept of god as a 'simple and lucid' explanation for the phenomena which otherwise he would be Unable to explain. Therefore, it is possible that man's evolution into a creative, innovative being provided the means by which the concept of god originated.

Science advances not by embracing new truths, but by a ruthless willingness to discard old ideas. If only the humans are "created in the image of God Then God is just an exalted man, who has "a body of flesh and bones. A new born is aware of two reflexes-one is scared of sound and two the height. The infant looks for protection from a terrifying impression of helplessness, for protection through love—which was provided by the parents It is god in the garb of parents.

We are living in the biotech century and genetic information has taken centre stage. Humanity will benefit from mapping the human genome.. Now Is There A GOD Gene? Frankly I don't know. At least one gene-VMAT2, controls emotions and consciousness. This is thought to be the "God gene". Now "Is there a God?" What we are is God's gift to us. What we become is our gift to God.

We are all accustomed to promises. We are also accustomed to seeing them made and broken. What can be said about God's promises to us? He has promised to supply every need we have but not the greed! That would include food, clothing, shelter, companionship, love, and salvation. It would not include the multiplicity of luxuries that we have come to think of as needs.

No, God has not left His name etched onto the surface of planets. However, there is abundant evidence that the universe was designed by super intelligent Agent, who purposed that the universe should exist and be capable of supporting advanced life. The design of the universe is just one line of evidence that God.

One belief is that God exists outside of time. We live in a universe of cause and effect. God has no need of being created, but, in fact, created the time dimension of our universe specifically for a reason - so that cause and effect would exist for us. However, since God created time, cause and effect would never apply to His existence.

Despite our scientific and technological brilliance, our understanding of God is often remarkably undeveloped—even primitive. There can never be a definitive version of a myth, because it refers to the more imponderable aspects of life. To remain effective, it must respond to contemporary circumstances.

Newton only gave a mathematical expression to the universal law of Gravity. Isaac Newton is today remembered as the greatest scientific genius who ever lived. His discoveries about light, physics, and mathematics have changed the world.

Newton has said "Gravity explains the motions of the planets, but it cannot explain who set the planets in motion. God governs all things and knows all that is or can be done."

Does God exist?

Both believers and atheists are constantly waiting for clear evidence to confirm or deny the existence of God. Just once I would love for someone to simply show you the evidence for God's existence or otherwise. No arm-twisting. No statements of, "You just have to believe.- You don't see the air you breath. You don't see the pain that hurts you. We believe in the existence of air and the pain. We are asked to accept god in the same way..

Marilyn Adamson puts forth the following facts clinch the issue that god exists.

The complexity of our planet points to a deliberate Designer who not only created our universe, but sustains it today.

Character and conduct

How does character differ from conduct?

Conduct is what we do! Character is what we are!

Conduct is the outward life; character is the life unseen, hidden within, yet evidenced by that which is seen.

Conduct is external, seen from without; character is internal-- operating within.

Character is the state of the heart; conduct is its outward expression.

Character is the root of the tree; conduct is the fruit it bears

All that is gold does not glitter and not all those who wander are not lost- Tolkien.JRR

Sometimes, reaching out and taking someone's hand is the beginning of a journey.

Some questions first,

What is the meaning of life?

What is the purpose of life?

Why is life limited?

Why is there a unique earth full of complex life in an enormous space?

Is there a life after end of this life?

Is there a design behind all of this? For a design you also need a designer!

There are so many questions. None of these have any answers. There are only hypotheses, conjectures, indirect evidences and lot more question and no definitive unquestionable answers. I feel i am lost in the wilderness of the journey of life. But i am findable. The saying 'Life is about the journey, not the destination', exaggerates the significance of destination. End of life is is the execution of life.

Before that final destination plan a journey and you do not reach or there are roadblocks then re-align to a new target if you need to.

Make Life a series of destinations.. A significance of the seed is to allow the perpetuation of organic life.

By the time most of us are adults we would be living out aide your home, may be in the hostels, PG accommodation, apartments etc. Life is most enjoyable and meaningful when you are present in every moment. Living in the past or future, as we often do, only serves to drain your spirit.

Our lessons come from the journey, not the destination.. We normally associate travel with boredom and tediousness. One day, after feeling really low and questioning my life choices, I had a revelation. I thought that perhaps it's possible for your dreams to serve you. Not only would this be a way to live out your passions in life, but also, the ride itself could serve as a way to shape the person you are continually becoming.

Why do we go to school, if not to graduate? Why do we exercise if not to be in shape? Why do we cook if not to eat the meal? The Journey is equally important! The journey is what makes the experience so unique.

BE where you are, even if it's not where you want to be! It's playing safe. Why not take the road less travelled sometimes. Dare to be special, dare to be different, and enjoy the journey. Adventure may hurt you but monotony will kill you.

Yes you need to be happy in life. Is it not a destination? The path chosen may not be for everyone, but it is an example of the importance of choosing your own path in life, and ignoring the pressure from family, friends, and society.

Is Success a Journey? And Not a Destination! It's what I desire. You would hardly find anyone who thinks otherwise. Success is the achievement of something that you intend. For some people success means achieving whatever they dream. For many it is the name, fame, ego, power, social acceptance and money.

Why Am I Here? –

So many searching for answers… No satisfying answers. Why am I here on earth? Where did I come from? What am I worth? Do I have any intrinsic value? Do I serve a purpose? These are all fundamental questions

Every man dies, not everyman really lives either.

In other words, why are we even born if we are only to die some 70 or 80 years later? Isn't there more to life than to say, "Eat, drink, and be merry for tomorrow we die?" Probably not if you believe the earth was created from a "Big Bang," that man evolved from amoebas millions of years ago, or that there is no Creator. Science is even discovering that the universe is getting old. It's dying, just like man, and it's not going to last forever. Something makes us wonder, "Why am I here?" That something is what? There is more to just living and dying.

Time is slipping by, like the sand in an hourglass. You have noticed that you need to do something before it's all over; Human society has been around for tens of thousands of years. Thousands of generations of humans have walked the earth.

Few billion humans have existed throughout history. Of those, very few have left traces of their existence, apart from a few bones maybe.

You should learn in early youth that your life is a journey, not a rest. You are travelling to the Promised Land, from the cradle to the grave, But we mortals, or most of us, are always in haste to reach nowhere, forgetting that the zest is in the journey and not in the destination. Sure the zest cannot be in the grave.

For some love is not a destination but a flight of fancy. The emotions run high but only between business/ power and ambition. Love is an intermission. They are forever on the hop.

Success is an event which is far too brief in the long journey of life. Religion is a medium you have selected to be in touch with god and depends on your beliefs. We cannot be happy all the time. God does not allow anyone to be happy all the time. He is worried if you will forget him. In order to keep you in the loop he ensures that happiness is a mirage. Education makes you complete. Yes you can be a learner all your life. This is not for all.

All do not have the urge to be lifelong learners.

Sometimes doubt is the opposite of faith, but sometimes doubt can be a pathway to faith.

Sometimes weakness is the opposite of strength, but sometimes weakness can be the pathway to strength.

Sometimes addiction is the opposite of sobriety, but sometimes addiction can be the pathway to sobriety.

Sometimes infidelity is the opposite of fidelity, but sometimes infidelity can be a pathway to fidelity.

Sometimes failure is the opposite of success, but sometimes failure can be the pathway to success."

— David W. Jones, Enough

If you woke up this morning with more health than illness, you are more blessed than the millions who will not survive this week. 500 million people in the world are in danger of terror and war and torture. Two of the three persons in the world go to bed hungry. Two billion people in the world cannot read or write. There is magnificence in our ordinary, everyday life. And, it is easy to miss beauty and significance when we are busy and inattentive. The possibility for hope, healing, and love in our world is real. Spiritual friends remind us – you belong, you matter. For this, let us be grateful..

Present day dilemmas.

We have lost the subtleness in our life. Everything is loud and crude. We are career oriented and have learnt to make a living but we hardly live. Man has reached the moon and machines have reached the Mars but we do not live like human beings should. Our market value has increased but we are guilty of lacking ethics and values.

We only talk and loud and hard only to be heard. We have lost the art of listening. We love ourselves more and seldom love others. We are intolerant and easily more than dislike others who are not in line with us. Modern technology has added years to life but have forgotten to add life to years. We are so self cantered that we are alien to even our neighbors.

The air we breathe is polluted and so is our soul. Now we write and map the Genome and sequence the DNA but we have not conquered the prejudice. We read more and learn less. We lay out large plans and accomplish less. We are always rushed and stressed. We do not have time to speak to the ailing parents. We have computers to store more and more but we communicate less and less.

We have forgotten the axiom 'food is laughter' now the axiom is laughter is medicine. We hardly smile but we rush to laughter clubs. It is time to remember that you are not properly dressed if you do not Smile. We drive recklessly and fail to see the the person lying on the road due to an accident. If we do stop it is only to take either a selfie or to take a photo for the papers. The road rage is on the increase.

The tempers we show is directly proportional to to the height of the apartments we live in. We spend more but we only buy less. Our purchasing power is as low as our ethical fiber. We spend more and enjoy less. We have more degrees and have less knowledge and even lesser compassion. We have money but less health and wellness. We lose our infancy, toddlerhood and grow up to be adults too soon and in no time we are senile . We rush to make money and ignore the health. Later we lose money to restore health. Most of us live as if we never die and later die as if we have never lived. We forget that A rich person is not the one who has the most but the one who needs the least. We forget that money cannot buy happiness and health. Money cannot buy love.

Darwin has stood the test of time. His theory of evolution is an accepted scientific document. Humans are on earth only for about 0.004% of the duration of the history of earth. Humans have evolved from a unicellular to a trillion cells being. That he is not dropped on earth just like that or has entered earth in the image of god. Human bodies are riddled with evidence to that effect.

The faulted and the one without- the flawless.

Criticism and contempt are highly destructive in loving relationships.. It renders the whole chemistry toxic. Contempt expresses the feeling of dislike toward a partner. Contempt is communication through insults and name-calling and eats away at a relationship rapidly and painfully.. if your relationship is truly toxic, then it may be time to leave. Prolonging the agony of a truly toxic situation will have deleterious effects.

In a relationship it does not matter who stumbles first. But it is important that one who gets up first must help the other person to get up as well. A great man when he makes a mistake, he realizes it. Having realized it, he admits it. Having admitted it, he corrects it. One who makes you realize your mistake is a teacher. it is the curse of all those who are powerful that they think it is not their fault.

If you are equal in the fault committees you should be equal in acceptance and realisation. You should not accept your faults just to prove that you have a big heart. It is that a fault denied is twice committed. The truth is that if you do not realize your fault it will grow every day and may become irreparable.

If a scientist commits a mistake it is not the fault of Science. Science cannot be faulted. When you are at fault it is easy to say I do not remember. But it is running away from the reality. God made the world beautiful, but humans made it a living hell. Go out in the morning, at the crack of dawn and you will see birds chirping, the parent birds going out and fetching food for their offspring, Elephant taking care of its younger sibblings, Tigers saving up food for the tigress and their offspring. Nature was meant to be beautiful but there was one flaw... humans. Human beings have emotions and emotions can be good or bad. Good emotions do no harm but bad ones do the harm.

In the present world a word of mouth does not carry any weight and contracts are required. The days of safe open spaces are gone, even doors are not enough but locks are required. Laws are not good enough but we need policing as many are outlaws. The literacy rates are up dispelling ignorance. But the worst wars are fought by most literate nations.

The governments have failed to govern. We may well accept the fact that we are far from perfect, but it is an in-built tendency of human nature to blame others for our faults. We are masters at making excuses.

Pleasure and pain are two ends of duality, two sides of the same coin, but they should not be taken as separate. They are one. Pleasure in itself will hold no attraction for you if you are not in pain. Joy is a movement from pain to pleasure.

Humanity has made some great strides in recent years. We can live longer than our ancestors, fly faster than the speed of sound, and access the world from a computer keyboard. But while we've progressed in some ways, we seem to be digressing in many others. Every decade, we see rise in crime, and violence, increase in the separations in marriage, and teenage attempts at ending their lives. Thousands of people around the globe contract HIV every day. Hundreds of millions of people experience chronic hunger and malnutrition. The list could go on. Humans can go that far and no further. it doesn't appear that we're doing a very good job of humanity. we still have lot of racial strife, and hunger and malnutrition. Therefore, wouldn't it be better to have a God who is greater. Think of the plethora of international charities – and then try to name more than one for old people. And though Unicef is a $4bn a year megalith at the heart of the UN establishment, there is no UN organisation for old people. Why the lack of concern? Is it because they die and perish sooner than later!

Frailty is failed aging- Chronic disease, Disability and Vulnerability. Challenge is to invoke prevention to promote robust aging.

Life is not about how far you can go, how high you can jump, or how much weight you can carry. Life is about experience, friendship, family, and the memories they leave with us. Why is it, that so many people are afraid of old age when the years enrich us? This presentation is a lovely reminder that no matter how old you may be, you should always be full of life, even more than when you were young.

Aging has the perceived stigma that we are becoming less useful members of society which can erode our confidence. Today's society has lost a huge part of its compassion. As a people, we've become desensitized to the core values we were taught in our younger days. As parents age, our own sense of reality is affected. The parents, who willingly helped us along the way, suddenly require our help. There is reversal of roles! Ageing is not a burden; older people can make valuable and important contributions to society, and enjoy a high quality of life. Good health is associated with access to green areas and the time spent outdoors.

Environmental threats such as pollution may also affect older people disproportionately. Airborne pollution is responsible for one of the heaviest burdens on public health systems.

Healthy eating is critical for seniors to remain independent and maintain their quality of life, and reduce the risk of developing chronic conditions such as high blood pressure, heart disease, respiratory diseases, and some cancers.

Physical activity brings multiple benefits and significantly contributes to healthy aging. Physical inactivity is associated with premature eclipse of life, chronic diseases, illness and disability, as well as reduced quality of life and independence. Tobacco use is the number one preventable cause of end of journey. Social support contributes to higher quality of life, increased life satisfaction and enhanced mental and physical well being.

Research has shown that healthy lifestyles are more influential than genetic factors in helping seniors avoid the deterioration traditionally associated with aging.

Purpose of life

Daily meditation for Purposeful living starts with calming the mind. We live in a world of distractions and discontent in the present moment. Contemplation is seeking answers to questions about who you are, how you should live, and where you belong.

What's the truth about life after life? Are we simply obliterated? Will we be punished for our earthly failures, rewarded for our good deeds? I have no answers. No one has returned to life from heaven or hell as the case may be! Living purposefully is one of the most effortless but enjoyable experiences which you can enjoy in life. When you are living purposefully life just flows Like flowing water. There are times when things can become turbulent.

Even though my body is not as young as it used to be I will never change my amazing friends, Things i have seen, lessons I have learnt and my loving family.

Are aware of the reason you were born on this earth. No you are not aware. Do you have an idea about your goals? Have you programmed your journey? That you are not aware does not prevent you from discovering the reason. Lack of knowledge of gravity does not prevent you from tripping.

Cleanse your mind of all the fake details thrust in you about god and purpose of your journey of life. A photograph can be an instant of life captured for eternity that will never cease looking back at you. Events come and go. The photographs are for life and beyond. Life is short. Eternity isn't. If you doubt me, ask a butterfly. Their average life span is a five to fourteen days.

So, live it to the fullest! Enjoy all that it has to offer. Life isn't about how many breaths you take in your life. It is about the number of moments that take your breath away. Nobody ever said life was easy but it is worth it.

How do you know what will happen tomorrow?

Research shows, you can't buy happiness. Everyone tries, of course…A beautiful house. Nice cars, Presents for the wife and kids and what not! These things may feel good for a little while… But eventually, they get old. And you start looking for a new house, a new car, and may not be a new wife and new toys for the family.

Your life is like the morning fog – it's here a little while, and then it's gone. We are used to everything having a beginning and an end. But eternal life isn't just something that starts after you die.

Eternal life is a life that is full and free and forever. It is peace, joy and assurance. It is comfort, strength and hope. It's never-ending life with God life in heaven after we die.

Most people think of eternal life as living forever in heaven. Eternal life means escaping the power of execution of life.. This life is ruled by death. Everything that lives will die. Physically, there is no way to escape it. So, one does not live after death. There is no life for eternity.

I think most of us think of eternity in the terms of years.. It is normal for us to think like that because our whole life is determined by time; seconds, minutes, hours, and days and years. We think of time like we think of the earth, it is a constant, something that never really changes. This is not the truth; it is just our feeble minds trying to comprehend something that we can't really get our minds around.

Einstein's Special Theory of Relativity predicted that time does not flow at a fixed rate: moving clocks appear to tick more slowly relative to their stationary counterparts. But this effect only becomes really significant at very high velocities that approach the speed of light.

When "generalized" to include gravitation, the equations of relativity predict that gravity, or the curvature of space-time by matter, stretches or shrinks distances depending on their direction with respect to the gravitational field and also will appear to slow down or "dilate" the flow of time.

But then eternity never ends. So can it still be measured in terms of long and short? It is silly to perceive eternity as long eternity and short eternity.

Time and Timelessness.

We are so caught up within the notion of time, our lives are overextended as we whirl and spin through time, sometimes experiencing endless turbulence and confusion - Time seems at the moment to be greatly speeded up. Time is linked to change. We perceive time to be an intense part of our lives because we perceive change happening so rapidly. Without the perception of change, we might not perceive time. - Night and day is one cycle which reminds us of the passage of time. So, too, are the changes of the moon. Larger cycles are the changes of the seasons. Our bodies are subject to constant change as we grow and age. I would want to bring in the old adage- Time and tide waits for none.

The feature of time we are most familiar with is that it passes, flowing by us whether we are willing to have it do so or not. We are born, we grow, we live, we learn from living, and eventually we die. So frankly i do not understand the concept of .timelessness.

The new identity available to us in this way is a fluid one which includes the perception of timelessness-within-time. We unfold like flowers within the landscape of space and time - budding, blooming, wilting, dying - and all parts of the passage are parts of our identity.

God is timeless- we are told time and again. Yes god exists. He is omnipresent. He created time and the creator cannot be the created.

Whose domain does the time belong to? To the Physicists or the philosophers! Is it in the arena of scientists? Simple it belongs to the clock! The clock is ticking relentlessly.

Human in Person

Is there a time limit for eternity? The clock tells the time of the day or night. Time is beyond anyone's hold. You cannot feel the time, it is not 'see'able, It is not saleable. We cannot feel the time except when it is boring . We cannot hear the time except the ticking of the clock. Then what is time?

Time is a funny thing. There never seems to be enough -- yet there is an infinite amount. Time slips through moments upon seconds into eternity. Time is past; yet present, to begin the future. Time waits for none. Science, the interpreter of the laws of nature and of the principles underlying them, cannot help us in our search to solve the mystery of time and space. The proper domain of Time is the universe.

Science and technology has only succeeded in measuring the smallest parts of time, time remains one of the great mysteries of the universe.. In the real world -- the world with time -- changes never stop. Change is constant.

Time was measured with the length of the shadow, recurring natural events like sunset, dawn, night onset, eclipse etc. That's how the timing of the time began!

Time only moves forwards. I have no idea if it can move backwards! No it cannot move from present to the past. We see people born and then grow old. They cannot grow young. Is god time? Answer is time is not god. One cannot be what one has created.

Each of us has only 24 hours a day and no one else can live our lives for us. This obvious yet profound fact means that time is potentially the major limiting factor in our personal lives. I know many people, I included, and who often feel have no time and who bemoan this limitation. Perhaps this attitude is a great mistake.

Time is priceless wealth in our life. One who doesn't care about time can never achieve his or her goals in his/her life. Everyone should know the value of time to get success in his or her life. Time plays a vital role in life.

We can mean two different things when we talk about time. It has always been assumed that clock time is absolute time. Einstein's theory Relativity has shattered that view.. A second type of time is sequence time. The next time, the last time, the first, second, third, etc. all express sequence time.

Is He limited to thinking the way we do? "For my thoughts are not your thoughts, neither are your ways are my ways," declares the LORD.As the heavens are higher than the earth, so are my ways higher than your ways and my thoughts than your thoughts.

This description of God is far removed from man's condition: "The length of our days is seventy years—or eighty, if we have the strength; yet their span is full of trouble and sorrow, for they quickly pass, and we fly away.

Count your age by the number of friends you have, not years. Count your life by smiles, not tears.—John Lennon

Again, because of our finite minds, we can only grasp the concept of God's timeless existence in part. And in so doing, we describe Him as a God without a beginning or end, eternal, infinite, everlasting.

Additionally, the science of physics tells us that time is a property resulting from the existence of matter. As such, time exists when matter exists. But God is not matter; God, in fact, created matter. The bottom line is this: time began when God created the universe. Before that, God simply existed. Since there was no matter, and because God does not change, time had no existence and therefore no meaning, no relation to Him.

Timelessness

Elegance is timeless. Absolute beauty is timeless. And I don't mean the kind of surface beauty that fades with age, or the sort of shallow wisdom that gets lost in platitudes.

What went before — let go of that! All that is to come — have none of it! Donot hold on to what is in between. Timelessness is the transcendence of time. There is no awareness of time at all, for there is no differentiation, and hence no change. Yesterday is but today's memory and tomorrow is today's dream.

Eternity is a term used to express the concept of something that has no end and/or no beginning. God has no beginning or end. He is outside the realm of time. Eternity is not something that can be absolutely related to God. God is even beyond eternity.

God is timeless rather than being eternally in time or being beyond time. Time was simply created by God as a limited part of His creation for accommodating.

TO Live or Exist

The world has never been a better place to live in and it will keep on getting better. We are better off now compared with 50 years ago. Urban living is a good thing for material comforts The world's cities now contain over half its people.

The rich get richer, but the poor do even better. The percentage of the world's people living in absolute poverty has dropped by over half. The United Nations estimates that poverty was reduced more in the past 50 years.

You don't have to do anything—you already exist. For those who merely exist Time loses meaning. Every day is just another day, another week, another month, another year. Life just slips away. To exist is to live As Though You Don't Exist You are no different from the inanimate objects around you as they exist until they are no longer needed.

Sadly though, far too many of us age much faster than we grow. Many of us wait for the right time. But one day we wake up and realize we're no closer than we were long ago. We find ourselves asking, "How did it get so late, and why haven't I moved? To exist is sleep-walking through life!

To live is to know the satisfaction of fulfilling that function/ purpose in life. I would rather go to bed knowing I made an impact in life, rather than going to sleep just being happy I survived another day. Live what you preach. Every day take one step that moves closer to your goal. Your ability to grow to your highest potential is directly related to your willingness to act. Make the world a better place--Jealousy is ugly. Be appreciative. Vow to get healthier. Big news for anyone born after the year 2000: They'll probably live to 100, according to research from Denmark. That's roughly 20 years longer than the life expectancy of the rest of us.

Success or failure in almost anything starts from within. Once you start believing in yourself, you create a domino effect of positive outcomes. Be less critical of others. Go-ahead and make yourself perfect before judging others. Inspire others to believe in you. Accept criticism and believe that others may have a different view. Tapping into pure self-confidence **your potential for success becomes exponential.** Talk less and Do More.

Why Is Life So Hard? Why life seems to be unfair?

Life is hard. But life is not impossible. Following are possible reasons that you may find daily life challenging. You've got a selfish streak in you. YOU are a hypocrite. **N**o one likes to be called a hypocrite. It's an insult—in all contexts And this fact makes life hard. You control your behaviour—but only to a point—and there are lots of evolved forces at work that control your behaviour along with whatever free will you've got.

We are all emotional Emotions have their upsides and their downsides. Negative emotions are deeply rooted in our evolutionary past—like it or not. And, yes, they make life hard. It's not always easy to get along. And this too makes life hard. How do we explain what we see in this world? Violence and attacks by terrorists, slavery, racism, world hunger? So why do bad things happen? **Why, Why?**

ife has always been meant to be tough and perceptibly hard. Yes it is not easy to live. May be we live to please others. That is how it becomes difficult and is hard on us. Is there a pattern to live which makes it smooth on you? There is no onen wayL that assures peace in life. Every life is different, circumstances are different, and reactions are different. So there is no set pattern to be at peace.

Have ever wondered why the life is so hard? Why is life unfair? We all feel the hardship is only on us. We feel everyone else is happy and comfortable. Some other guy made it through the door and you didn't? Why not me/ Did you ever look at someone and think, "He is so lucky. He has money, he's in a great relationship and wow -- what a great career, being able to travel like that?

Why me? What have i done? No answer/ the astrologer tells you your imagined misdeeds in the previous life or some Vaasthu mistakes in your house and sets you on fire after making a nice buck! We wear the mantle of martyrdom and try to find solace. We blame everyone except ourselves for the misery and suffering. There is no question that there is pain and intense suffering in this world. Some of it is explained by selfish, hateful actions on the part of others. Some of it defies an explanation in this life from one's own self.

Take an honest look at yourself. Think about your attitudes. We simply persist on a particular path when life is telling us to go another way. Are you being stubborn? No one likes to be told they are arrogant. Trying to swim against the current is difficult. But it is the fish that go with the flow. It is bound to make the life rocky. If you are wrong do you admit ? Are you open to change the course on the way or midway? Can you recognise the source of trouble or does your stubbornness and ego prevent you. This is arrogance, plain and simple. Often difficulties are simply life's way of telling you that you need to change. Your life would be so much easier and enjoyable if you'd just listen to what it is trying to tell you. Humble yourself and listen.

Inexperience

Life has to be lived forwards. The Past is called the experiences. The act of living forward is so varied and unpredictable. Life can sometimes seem much harder. You may be facing things you haven't had to deal with before and that you lack preparation to handle. This can certainly make life seem laborious and painful. Just because you lack experience doesn't mean that you have to wallow in it.

Take the bull by the horns and get some help to ease the trouble you are facing. Things will smooth out once you do. The past experiences need not repeat and many times they don't. It is altogether a new issue to be dealt as it comes.

The question "Why?" as regards the unfairness of life is often at its most basic level not a question at all. Rather it is a statement. The statement is something like this: "What happened to me is unfair. I don't deserve this. I am angry about this. No explanation about why this happened to me would be good enough, because it is not fair. I won't let go of being angry until somebody, until God, fixes this. I am just going to be angry, because what happened to me is unfair."

Why did God make the earth and us? He doesn't really need us, so why did he create anything?

God said on the first day-"Let there be light," and there was light '.God called the light a "day", and the darkness he called "night". So there was darkness pervading before the ray of light could peep in. Science has measured the speed of light. But what is the speed of darkness? Any answers!

So god created Day and night and the earth. He created the man and the woman to inhabit the earth and called them Adam and Eve. They were created in the image of god and were very different from his other creations. He gave them knowledge, wisdom and intelligence. Then God said, "Let us make man in our image, in our likeness, and let them rule over the fish of the sea and the birds of the air, over the livestock, over all the earth, and over all the creatures that move along the ground.' Man and woman were made by God to look after all the earth, which he had just completed. He created rules to rule and called it Law.

Learned jurists toast the majesty of the law. Politicians swear by its sanctity asserting that it will take its due course. But seasoned criminals are thoroughly familiar with its loopholes. They know how to flout the law and yet how to survive by it. But those who have felt the slings and arrows of misapplied law unhesitatingly subscribe to the Charles dickensian dictum 'The Law is an ass.'

Probably, the highest tribute ever paid by Charles Dickenson! Law commands respect only from the law-abiding.

Life is unfair.

You're right, it is unfair. It's beyond absurd. 40% of the wealth is owned by 1% of the population. A fair world is just not possible.

Why life is unfair? Because we believe that it's unfair. The delusion of fairness makes unfair that much more uncomfortable. Life's unfair. And the sooner you realize it, the better People know you by your actions and not by your perception of yourself. You may be the most creative person to yourself, but unless people get to see your creations, your self-evaluation (which is often being the best in the world) holds zero value.

It seems so incredibly unfair at times. One person has plenty; the other person barely scrapes by. That woman next door has ideal health; that man in the corner over there is weak and feeble. One kid has the perfect home, the perfect parents, the perfect school; some teenager has run away from home, living on the streets or at a rescue mission, questioning what went wrong. Some questions remain questions, at least for the time being. And that's hard.

A disturbing trend of martyrdom is taking hold with people feeling entitled to behave selfishly because they feel theyhave been wronged by society and this culture is becoming a widening phenomenon. This culture makes for worse citizens - people who are less helpful, more entitled and more selfish.

Life has been fair to very few people in this world. So what? Accept that life is unfair! Who said it was meant to be fair. In fact it is fair to those who are powerful and flout the rules at will. It is fair to those who can bend it like Beckham.

To think that life is fair is irrational. This specific distortion of our thoughts is called the doctrine of Fairness. It basically says that somewhere in our head, we sometimes think like a kid that all of life "should be fair riding on some fantasy. A baby's life depends on taking the first breath and the first cry. It depends on the breast milk. As it grows it has to learn to share, share the toys, love food and everything else .It has to survive the not so clean water, and communicable diseases. Yes the life goes on.

Difficult events may lead us to think life came to mean nothing, because everything in it had brought me nothing but trouble. It had all been useless; I had been chasing the wind Bad things happen to good people.

Every day, we have abundant opportunities to recognize injustice, on scales large and small, in our own lives and the lives of people we love. We do, however, need to accept that our response to perceived wrongs affects our ability to right them.

Life is about passion, freedom and love. I will only walk this road once; I might as well make the most of it. Live your life. Do not just merely exist. Just when you think it can't get any worse, it can. And just when you think it can't get any better, it does. If you don't know where you are going, any road will get you there. I am torn between a desire to improve the world and a desire to enjoy the world. This makes it hard. Never tell your problems to anyone...20% don't care and the other 80% are glad you have them.

What would i do if destiny twisted the road i took? What if it threw me to a place I did not want to go? Would you fight, would run or would I accept? Set across these dilemmas I conclude 'Life is what you make of it'. What is the point of life, when we come to the end?" I wonder. It seems like, even though there's an abundance of goodness in our lives, the prevalent theme seems to be this struggle to find balance, peace and happiness.

What is the meaning of it all? What is the purpose of life? I asked silently in the privacy and serenity of my thoughts. I reflected on my own experiences—particularly my own "blind" chase towards a more promising tomorrow. "All this chasing -for what?" I asked myself.

The art of medicine consists in amusing the patient while nature cures the disease Certainly there are things in life that you can't buy with money, but it's very funny - Did you ever try buying them without money-?

The entire chase is to earn money and more money, to become more famous, for recognition and to be worshipped. Praise is what one is looking for! When will I ever make it to Rich and famous group? But will that day ever arrive? The wanting for more never ends; and happiness will always elusive! If you're chasing money you'll be running all your life, if you're chasing dreams you'll be sleeping all your life.

With money you can buy a house but not a home, with money you can buy a clock but not time, with money you can buy a book but not knowledge, with money you can buy blood but not life, With money you can buy physical intimacy but not love.

When you're young you push through life making choices without thinking of repercussions and consequences! Suddenly you start wondering how you got there where you are.

Life reminds us of the impermanency of our human existence, and the preciousness of the time we are wasting on mundane things.

Running away from any problem only increases the distance from the solution. The Easiest way to escape from a problem is to solve it.

Life will always remain a gamble. In three words I can sum up everything I've learned about life- It goes on!

Have you tried doing things outside the box? Yes you may find solace and return to the mainstream later. The world is a complex and beautiful place with a wide spectrum of possibilities, and full of unpredictable opportunities. Your life is your masterpiece. You are with a huge Canvas and you are the painter. Go ahead and live.

Philosophy to Live is by - Live and let live is the spontaneous non-aggressive co-operative behaviour. Smile every chance you get. Not because life has been easy, perfect, or exactly as you had anticipated, but because you choose to be happy and grateful for all the good things you do have and all the problems you know you don't have.

In a world where you can be anything you want, BE YOURSELF. To Live Life is to share your happiness! Live and let live is one of the keys to peace in our lives. When we practice tolerance in our lives we are liberated to work on our own issues. Two human beings cannot exactly be the same in physical structure or in mental makeup.

The world is a dangerous place to live not because of the people who are evil but because of the people who don't do anything about It. Life is not fair. Get used to it. The real world won't care about your self-esteem. The world will expect you to accomplish something before you feel good about yourself. Before you were born, your parents weren't as boring as they are now. They got that way paying your bills; cleaning your room and listening to you.

Can there be a life without mistakes? Yes one who leads a perfect life. One who has attained Perfection? No life will be monotonous. What are these mistakes for? Is it as a lesson or as an experience? How many times one is allowed to make before he learns a lesson out of it? Your misery is optional.

Remember that the best relationship is one in which your love for each other exceeds your need for each other.. When adults make most of the decisions and rules we deprive our kids of the opportunity to become responsible. They need that responsibility given to them to be able to develop life 's ways and means. It's good to learn from your mistakes. It's better to learn from someone else's mistakes.

You don't have to win every argument. Agree to disagree. Think with your brain, act with your heart. Give a lot, but don't lose yourself is Machiavelli's principle that "the ends justify the means". Forgiving terrorists is left to God. But fixing their appointment with God is our responsibility.

It requires sunlight, water and manure for the flower to bloom and give fragrance. Respect those people who find time for u in their busy schedule. But love those people who never see their schedule when you need them."

Live for someone who lives for you. The hardest moments are not those when tears flow from your eyes, it's when you have to hide those tears in your eyes with a smile to remove the tears from someone else's eyes.

Never stop your smile even if you're sad because you never know who likes your smile. For the world you may be just someone, but for someone you may be the world. People have always tried to take you down. Just because someone's opinion is valued by many doesn't mean they are always right. Many people won't like what you have to say, how you present yourself, or what you do. But many others would have liked all these.

Accept that the world is not perfect. I accept I am not. You don't have to go around hating and making others feel your pain. If you expended energy on everyone you hated, you'd be finished, fast. There are too many people in the world to try to limit diversity so why bother. Live and let live.

I arise in the morning torn between a desire to improve the world and make it a better place to live. I have a undeniable desire to enjoy the world. This makes it hard to plan the day. Thinking is not to agree or disagree but to see the truth.

Fill what's empty. Empty what's full. Scratch where it itches. I believe living life is like licking honey off a thorn- One should not think of retiring from the world until the world will be sorry that you are going to retire.

In life all of us have an unspeakable secret, an irreversible regret, an unreachable dream and an unforgettable love. To succeed in life, you need three things: a wishbone, a backbone and a funny bone. Miracle is not to walk either on water or in thin air, but to walk on earth. Every day we are engaged in a miracle which we don't even recognize: When you are busy, stressed or otherwise distracted - do not forget to live. Do not forget to make sure that you leave yourself time to enjoy life.

To live also means to care for your life - as I mentioned, not squander it. Be aware of what you are doing to your mind and body. You do not need be obsessed with it to the point of boredom, but gently be aware of what you eat, drink. Be aware of what lacking sleep will do to it. Having a healthy body makes you a great deal more capable of happiness, sleeping well, confidence, thinking clearly.

It makes all of these concepts, living, loving, learning, respect and responsibility much easier than if you have not looked after your body. Above all – take responsibility for living - for your life. Too often we go through life having each day pass like the one before it.

This is a preposterous statement. I have seen the opposite happen. The crime and cruelty gets rewarded. Virtues and values are punished. I have seen this happening so many times that I believe this the rule.

The key to doing what you are passionate about and living the life of your own choosing is to overcome your own fears and many of the socially-reinforced beliefs that our parents, friends, and school teach us. To begin discovering what you really want out of life and what's truly possible, you must question all of your assumptions.

Believe that you are capable of making good decisions on your own. Be patient with your mistakes. Develop persistence. Listen to the opposition but don't let it stop you. Live on your own terms. Don't wait for anyone else to do it. Expect the progress to be slow if you have been living on others' terms for most of your life thus far.

Living on your own terms" should never be an excuse for hostile or grossly irresponsible behaviour. Remember that the best relationship is one in which your love for each other exceeds your need for each other.

Have you ever noticed how there are areas of your life which you might consider private and nobody else's business. The ONLY reason to get married and/or have kids is because you want to, not because your family have nagged you into it, not to provide some kind of security blanket for yourself, not because it's 'expected' and most definitely not to prove a point.

Life is about living, loving, learning and of course laughter. Living life on life's terms has much to do about our attitude toward our life. Our life is all about change and choice. Simplicity is the ultimate sophistication. Simply do the work you love and love the work you do! Time is ticking. We've been separating work and play since we were kids. The stuff that you 'had' to do and the stuff that you never wanted to do was work, and the stuff that you wanted to do was playing or 'free time'.

This is why subjects such as Art, Theatre, and Music aren't considered 'real' majors. No one goes to college to major in 15th Century French Poetry because of all of the wonderful job opportunities. They did it because they loved it.

Critical Thinking is actually a useful ability absorbing important information and using that to form a decision or opinion of your own—rather than just spouting off what you hear others say. We are exposed to so much information and so many different opinions every day that it's really easy to get lost in the details.

Most of us have a hard time accepting criticism without getting hurt or angry or defensive … and just as many of us have a hard time giving criticism without making others hurt or angry or defensive. People don't often take criticism well, even if it is done for good reasons. Many people assume what they say or do is right, and that the criticism is wrong. They don't like to hear that they are wrong. Well perceived suggestions are well received than criticism. Much criticism is negative. That hurts the discussion, because things can take an ugly turn from there. Be genuinely positive. This keeps the discussion positive, and people are more likely to receive it in a positive way. Never criticize the person. Always criticize the actions.

Taking criticism can be a difficult thing. Criticism is a form of communication. The right kind of criticism can give you an advantage. Use positive language, Don't take it personally.

Never outsource your thinking. Be a voice, not an echo. (Albert Einstein.) meaning, say what you feel is right, I believe we all have a voice that is far more important than we could ever imagine. It leaves a footprint and creates a page in our book of life. It is easier said than done, but that is what faith is. I for one am still making mistakes and learning every day, but progress is the goal, not perfection.

I'm developing a new obsession: Originality, Trying to be different and unique. Originality cannot be taught; it cannot be passed on from one to another. Neither can creativity. But they can be encouraged, they can be nurtured.

Take back your thinking. Decide for yourself. There's no massive amount of effort here. It's a choice. Decide that you'll think for yourself on these matters and you'll be a lot happier. Pause for a moment and ask yourself: How many new, unique, original thoughts have you had today? Our lives are designed around routines. I wake up every day in the same bed, in the same house with the same person. I have a great life but my life is also very structured – so it's no wonder that my mind is not fizzing every day with new ideas.

New ideas are delightful. Think of a time when you captivated by a thought or idea that you had never had before. Original ideas are not usually thunderbolts from out of the blue. Originality must be nurtured and stimulated. You cannot force a new thought, but you can create the right conditions to generate the sparks and seeds of a new idea. Never change your originality for the sake of others as no one can play your role better than you. So be you. You are the best.

We are all created equal. I went with the flow and rarely stood up for what I believed in. Through faith I was able to see that I was following the path of least resistance and walking a path that was not my own. I was simply an echo, and not a voice.

I believe we all have a voice of our own. It is easier said than done, but that is what faith is. I for one am still making mistakes and learning every day, but progress is the goal, not perfection. If we cannot speak up and voice who we are, then what do we stand for? What are we doing with our lives?

The credit card industry exists to lend us money in order to keep us in debt and line its pockets with interest payments. That's how the system is set up and if you play by those rules, you'll be forever trying to crawl out of a hole that was designed to get deeper faster than you can climb.

If you want something and there are too many gates in your way, don't waste your life trying to convince their keepers to open them for you, everywhere you look and see a success story, you almost always see old rules being substituted for new ones. Remember that not getting what you want is sometimes a wonderful stroke of luck.

To be kind to yourself, you need to be wrong sometimes. You need to be ok with being wrong and you should be ok when others around you are wrong. That means going against the grain and speaking your mind, especially when it's different from what those around you are thinking.

Striving to be wrong forces you to be a more creative thinker, someone who is not tied down by the status quo and how things are typically done. These are the people who, ask the "why's" and ask the "why not's." People who fear being wrong generally end up adopting group or herd mentality. Never outsource your thinking! That's why He gave you a brain! Use it!

Do We Have to Die? is it a choice, and the only reason we die is because we believe that it is inevitable. The cause of end of life is said to be simply that we believe in it and it is inevitable., I am of the firm belief that it is foolish to aspire for immortality. Do we need immortality? It would be a torture to live with the physical body with all the ailments, and the body not able to support all the systems. Probably with this imperfect body after a time one would be begging for relief in the form of finality of life- to yhe grave! It is not possible to live forever. One dies because it is the final destination of the journey of life.

Exactly how far and how fast life expectancy will increase in the future is a subject of some debate, but the trend is clear. An average of three months is being added to life expectancy every year and experts estimate there could be a million centenarians across world by 2030. To date, world's longest-living person on record lived to 122 anfd in Japan alone there were more than 44,000 centenarians in 2010. Some researchers say, however, that the trend towards longer lifespan may falter due to an epidemic of obesity now spilling over from rich nations into the developing world. Immortality is the power not to die. Radical life extension, curing aging, super longevity all mean to look beyond the past of dying to a future of unlimited living. Man is the Cosmic Orphan. He is the only creature in the universe who asks, "Why?" Other animals have instincts to guide them, but man has learnt to ask questions.

There is one subject about which we are as ignorant as our forebears, and that is destination of life.. For most of us, our ignorance is a fact of life. We either accept what is inevitable mystery or ignore its inevitability. Why die? Why not live forever?

The human body grows up and then starts growing down, eventually to die. Why do we have to die? Why do we have to deteriorate as we grow old?

One of my favourite quotes comes from Stendhal: "Life is too short, and the time we waste in yawning never can be regained."Your time is limited; don't waste it living someone else's life. Don't be trapped by dogma, which is living the result of other people's thinking. Don't let the noise of other's opinion drown your own inner voice. And most important, have the courage to follow your heart and intuition, they somehow already know what you truly want to become. Everything else is secondary.

Make the best a life that is short.

Caste and Cash Rules Everything around Me. Money is the cause of and solution to life's most unnecessary problems. Gossip is the worst. Life is just too short to worry about the lust lives of others. The less you worry about work, the quicker it goes by. Never be ashamed of who you are or what you do to earn a living. You are not defined by your career; you define it.

Sooner or later in your life, you are going to have to face the inevitability of your own termination of life. The end is not easy to face; you cannot dodge the grim reaper. Have more courage and tenacity. Face mortality, and go live your life. It's never too late to start over. If you weren't happy with yesterday, try something different today. Don't stay stuck. Do better.

People have no time anymore to call their friends and to spend time with them, but waste hours of their valuable time online, on Face book – checking status messages, addictively playing games, chatting with random strangers or watching videos on YouTube. You can hear people mumble I am in a rush or have not got any time!" while they rush from their workplaces to their entertainment stations, called home.

Anything Outside Your Control, my mantra is when life gets too stressful is, "this too shall pass and this is only temporary. The general idea is to stop yourself from getting annoyed about that which is outside your control. Death and taxes are far from the only guarantees in life. You'll have a hard time in life without paying bills. Bills are relentless.

Experience the moment fully. Live life to the full – one moment at a time. Be Better, Not perfect - Striving too much for perfection will spoil your life. It will wipe out all those little imperfections which are making you... human. Being better, on the other side, is rewarding. Look back at the yesterday just say: I'm better! Stop Being Judgmental - Excessive criticism will ruin your enthusiasm.

You only live once, and life is short. Live fully. One who has lived his life will not have the fear of the end of life. People who smile in public have been through every bit as much as people who cry, frown, scream, etc. They just have the courage and strength to smile through it.

Do not compromise your values. Don't compromise on your ethics. Trust your instincts. Do whatever you want so long as you can look yourself in the mirror. Be charitable. It's never too late to start over. If you weren't happy with yesterday, try something different today. Don't stay stuck. Do better. Keep an open mind. Learn to forgive.

Stay healthy, eat right, and most importantly, be kind to all. Pray, meditate, forgive yourself, appreciate others. Trust yourself. Trust your own strengths. Make peace with your yesterday so that it will not compromise either today or tomorrow of your life. Know that time heals and give time.

Do not ask too many questions! You are not required to know all the answers on all the questions. A Bad day is not a bad life! Patience is golden. Still it is true that patience does not cook a stone. Now sky is not the limit as there are foot prints already in the Moon. Every day is a new beginning. Fight your fears and live your dreams.

Is Immortality Possible?

How much money would you pay to live forever keeping in mind that forever is a long time; you could certainly arrange some kind of long-term loan, since you'd have plenty of time to make the payments.

If we can get a handle on how to prevent cellular aging, in theory, we can extend life, potentially indefinitely. We may also be able to fight cancer, since the cellular mechanism involved in this fatal disease is closely related to that in aging. In fact, cancer is a type of cell that simply doesn't die. That's why it's so hard to treat. This wouldn't be a problem, except that cancer cells also divide uncontrollably and invade the healthy cells around them.

Evolution of Life expectancy shows how the life expectancy continues to rise over time, and shows this trend over the past 60 years during which life expectancy in the developed world went up about 12 years. It is possible for the life expectancy to rise faster than time goes by, so that it would rise 5 or more years for every 5 years gain in technology.

Why Life Needs an end?

Is heaven place only for pious and the good and Hell for the outrageous and the bad?

You were not afraid to be born; why be afraid to die? It is the same thing. You cannot avoid it by getting scared. You are only making it difficult!

Life after the end is the science of human decomposition. Does everything about a person disappear at the termination? The body Sure, it's gone, the brain? It stops working, and then dissolves, But what about awareness? There are no scientifically proven answers.

Our attitudes and beliefs regarding end of life have a great influence on our approach to life. There is perhaps no greater grief than being parted from a loved one by his oe her end1. Two of the big questions religions have sought to answer over the years are: "Why does life exist as we know it?" and "What happens after we die.

We do not have a "right to die. We neither have a right to birth. We cannot choose our own parents. We do not know when and where we die! "A "right" is a claim. We do not have a claim. Rather, we just have to submit ourselves. We do not and should not decide, when our life will end, any more than we decided when it began. Only those who voluntarily end their life probably know when to end their life.

Much less does someone else -- a relative, a physician, or a legislator--decide when our life will end. None of us is master over life and its end. We have no right to terminate life. the science of ageing has progressed by leaps and bounds in recent decades, and I have little doubt that gerontologists will eventually find a way to avoid, or more likely delay, the unpleasantness of extended life that some say are about to disappear, but which as anyone with their eyes open realises is occurring with increasing frequency.

This question is similar to asking why there is sunrise and sunset. The sun sets because for the purpose of rising. If it wasn't for the sun we wouldn't be able to distinguish between light and shadow. So same way, there is no evolution without the end. For the process of evolution, something or some species must die and perish so that the new one comes. Like the old saying; "The old should make way for the new!"

A lot of people are scared by the fact that their life now is all they'll ever get, and dying isn't viewed by most as a pleasant experience, therefore people don't want to die. People are not aware of life after life. They are afraid .

Does the finality of death make life meaningless?

Is life a travel from nothingness to nothingness? When we die, we won't remember anything we ever accomplished. It's as if it never happened. As long as we still have to die someday, the MAIN reason for living now should be to kill death." ~David Pizer.

Everyone dies, but almost no one really lives. I am glad that I was born into this world. I appreciate this wonderful opportunity called LIFE and I lament the possibility that it might come to an abysmal end — blackness — lights out! Sayonara to life!

"I do not fear death. I had been dead for billions and billions of years before I was born, and had not suffered the slightest inconvenience from it." **Mark Twain"**

I regard the brain as a computer which will stop working when its components fail, he said in the interview. There is no heaven or afterlife for broken down computers. That is a fairy story for people afraid of the dark." Stephen Hawking.

End is one of those things nobody wants to think about. It seems, almost, as if everyone just walks around pretending like it does not exist. Something binds the topics of the end and meaning. The end has always been inevitable, but the idea that science will eventually conquer the end has taken root due to a combination of future technologies like nanotechnology, genetic engineering.

Some think the possibility of technological immortality renders human life meaningless.

It makes life more meaningful because you know it will end. You have to make the best of the time that you have, before it runs out. The end has nothing to do with making life meaningful or otherwise. The way you LIVE makes life meaningful or not. Dying is just the end of the ride on this planet.

Where do people go after the end of their life?! Nobody has returned for sure as of now. It is believed that god made man from the dust and man returns to the dust. Afterwards it is hypothetical interplay of mind and soul. It is theorized that Mind belongs to the brain and soul to the heart. The heart and the mind belong to the body and die after cessation of breathing. Do good people go to heaven after dying and bad to hell? The answer is a firm –NO. Both go to their graves and some on to the pyre. To the question if the devils exist- the answer is a No. it is only a psychological derangement.

In 1977 Dr Osis published- At the Hour of death, including reports from over 1,000 physicians and nurses in India as well as the United States. It reported on the dying of more than 100,000 people. He has narrated many near death experiences, all are like stories which are not verifiable. Birth and the end, the inseparable fact of all life on earth, should not be a secret to man. Everything, positively everything, speaks for the probability of an existing world of other substance, which the average person of today is unable to see. Life after life is life in heaven/ hell.

Life is hard. Then you die. Then they throw mud in your face. Then the worms eat you. Be grateful it happens in that order.. Many that live deserve die and some die that deserve to live. Can you give it to them, fearing for your own safety? Even the wise cannot see all ends.

And when the soul departs, it goes somewhere, of course. There are two destinations: one is a place of unending joy, happiness, pleasure and eternal bliss, etc. There is no pain, sorrow, regret or evil in that place. That place is heaven – God's abode. Heaven is the place for enjoying good comfortable ambience. All those who have never enjoyed life in their sojourn on earth and who have lived for others will go there.

The second is a place of torments and torture, anguish, regrets and indescribable pain The Hell. All those who have lived their lives to the hilt, who have been self cantered will be lodged in hell. So hell is a place where you are likely to get the best of company.

Who deserves to go to heaven or end up in hell? Whether or not a person goes to any one of the two places mentioned depends entirely on his or her karma- the way one has lived during his/ her lifetime. That means that based on our own merits -Our own morality, kindness, philanthropy, goodness, religiosity or whatever any good thing will qualify us for heaven.

Albert Einstein: I Cannot Conceive of an Individual Surviving Physical Death

I cannot conceive of a God who rewards and punishes his creatures, or has a will of the kind that we experience in ourselves. Let feeble souls, from fear or absurd egoism, cherish such thoughts. I am satisfied with the mystery of the eternity of life and with the awareness and a glimpse of the marvellous structure of the existing world, together with the devoted striving to comprehend a portion, be it ever so tiny, of the Reason that manifests itself in nature. - Albert Einstein in -The World As I See It.

Me and my professional life!

When asked to describe my life, I often reply, "It is an organized chaos." I have lived full and fruitful life as a cardiac surgeon and now as Vice Chancellor of one of the biggest universities. This makes for a very fulfilling and rewarding life. The rewards of this profession are profound.

Heart surgery requires technical finesse, decisiveness, adaptability, and physical stamina. We as heart surgeons start the day with "a full plate" and things are continuously added. Academic deadlines research deadlines, emergencies, long operations, and family needs compete for our time. At the end of the day, it is tremendously rewarding when you can explain to your wife and children as to how you saved someone's life. I know that I am a better surgeon because I am a good father and now a grand one at that, and I am similarly a much better father because I am a cardiac surgeon.

I will state the reasons why I became a cardiothoracic surgeon, and why I believe it remains a viable, exciting, stimulating, challenging, and rewarding specialty for young physicians. I made the decision to become a physician when I was 15 years old. My sister underwent an emergency caesarean section and I was so impressed with the surgeon and the others who cared for my sister that I decided then and there that I wanted to be a surgeon. The surgeon was a quiet, compassionate, but highly efficient individual who was totally dedicated to her profession. She loved her work and her patients.

It was a fascinating experience and I was hooked! This fascination with cardiopulmonary perfusion and its physiology remains with me to this day, some 30 years later. That a human being can be connected to a Heart-Lung machine, stop the heart and lungs and have his or her Heart and respiratory functions totally performed by a machine for up to three or four hours, have a major cardiac condition corrected, and emerge from anaesthesia physiologically intact -is nothing short of a miracle. Today these miracles have become routine without stopping the heart.

Would I become a cardiothoracic surgeon if I had it to do over again? In a heartbeat! Yes of course.

If you are a student or resident with intelligence, drive, and stamina, who loves challenges, hard work and positive outcomes, If you are result-oriented, If you love working with your hands as well as your brain, and enjoys caring for others and interacting with highly competent physicians you should strongly consider becoming a cardiothoracic surgeon. As I retrospect the three years of my tenure as a Vice Chancellor, I am fond of Charlesdiken's famous Utterances, "It was the best of times; it was the worst of times.

I was an accidental but not an exceptional choice, an awkward – and, above all an unlucky – vice-chancellor. I took over as VC on 3rdFeb 2009 and I have my term up to Feb. 2013. Accidental because I never imagined I would be a vice-chancellor and that too of Bangalore University. My right of passage, as a professor and then as the Director of SJIC was with reference to Health University.

Vice Chancellors- I have always thought were members of a strange tribe, idealistic and pretentious in equal measure.

Most vice-chancellors I thought are born and bred in the academic system of the university. I was and I am – the product of a very different world, chaotic but committed, idealistic and sociable world of medicine, cardiology and cardiac surgery.

And I was an awkward vice-chancellor, because I have always seen myself as a rebel. I am always comfortable with being a leader. I have always loved arguments and winning them. The management "cult"– leaves me cold.

But, above all, I am not a lucky vice-chancellor. Yes the Examination reforms were a major success. None of my predecessors had ventured into this mine field. However, there have been challenges from student and staff activism and their resistance to the "reforms".

Vice-chancellors are not simply agents of their councils and boards; nor only leaders of executive teams. They are expected to and should exercise–leadership. They must lead the whole university– not simply today's students and graduates but also future generations with their ideals intact; not just today's staff, but tomorrow's and yesterday's. Universities have identities, values, even souls, not just "brands" or key performance indicators.

It is said that the journey of a thousand miles begins with a step. Since I took that first step, we have been marching forward, addressing emergent issues, providing leadership, creating programmes, promoting scholarship, advancing professionalism and training, and doing the best that we can .

Yes I am proud of my university –The Bangalore University and to be its Vice Chancellor. My mission is to make a positive difference in the career and lives of Bangalore University Students and the faculty. I have never separated the life I live from the words I speak. I am always ready to learn, but I do not always like being taught.

I harbor no illusions that the task ahead will be an easy one; but neither do I harbour fears that they are insurmountable; I instead harbour hope, a resounding hope, that with determination, dedication, and zeal I will succeed.

However feebly I met these challenges at Bangalore University, I was always aware of it. Making sense of these intellectual dynamics in a concrete social and institutional context is immeasurably more difficult than "re-engineering" or "re-branding". But why else would you want to be a vice-chancellor?

I harboured no ill will towards anyone in the university including the ones who created unrest, an atmosphere of intolerance and intolerance in the campus. All this is happening at the behest of few outside the university. I feel sorry for them that they do not seem to know the extent of disruption they have caused to the university and the damage of course to me personally- I have been slapped with an atrocity case for doing my work. Living is too hard right now.

On a day such as this one, we must celebrate for what the university has achieved over its Sixty four years of existence; reflect on the sacrifices of those before us and indeed reaffirm the dedication to the pursuant of the noble mission that constitutes the cornerstone of the existence of this cherished university. Uphold the dignity.

Adieu to Bangalore University

Dear Friends,

I am extremely grateful to His Excellency the Governor of Karnataka and Chancellor of all the Universities of the state of Karnataka for his kind support, advice and guidance during my tenure as The Vice Chancellor of Bangalore University. His Excellency has stood by me during crisis periods. It was indeed my Privilege to have served under him.

I am grateful to the former Chief Minister Shri Eddyurappa who chose me to be appointed as the Vice-chancellor of one of the biggest universities in Asia. I am indebted to the present Honourable CM shri jagadish shettar for his kind support and making me the chairman of Karnataka state health commission.I thank Shri Jamal, Shri Gurumatt and Shri Ramakrishna IPS, immensely for being with me all the time.

I thank my office staff in particular for their help and cooperation. I thank one and all in the University.I thank the media- both print and electronic for your kindness and generosity in giving wide coverage - in the last several months.

Given the turbulence every day for the last ten months this day could have come any day. The day has finally arrived four months and a few days too soon - four years of my term as Vice Chancellor is to be over in Feb2013.There is a time for everything - and today is the time for me to go. I am leaving with a cloud in my heart and mind.

The indifferent gaze is a perpetual farewell- Malcom de Chazal

I don't cry because it's over. I Smile because it happened. I was and I am – the product of a very different world, committed, idealistic and sociable world of medicine, cardiology and cardiac surgery. I have never separated the life I live from the words I speak. I strongly believe that conditioning of the students mind to fit a particular ideology, whether political or religious, breeds enmity between man and man. Regimentation and prejudice are being cultivated and enforced. I believe Vice-chancellors are not simply agents of university's academic councils and syndicate bodies. VC's are over and above all that.

I took over as VC on 3rdFeb 2009 and from nowhere in 2009 to 13th in 2010, to 9th in 2011- amongst all the six hundred universities in India.

What the Bangalore University has achieved in these three and a half years through reforms offering thousands of students their results in time to pursue post graduate studies or professional careers who almost certainly would have missed the bus due to late announcement of results previously- is a truly life- changing experience, that cannot adequately be put into words. I am glad and proud to have played a major role in that.

We were hoping to break into top five universities in India.

I was working hard towards that.

In the recent past Life as a Vice chancellor for me was like a truck hitting me from behind while I was walking /dreaming about how to get the university into the top five bracket in India.

No it was not to be!

From 9th to 20th in 2012amongst Indian universities in Six months! From First to Third in Karnataka! What a fall!! No I am not blaming anybody. Making sense of these intellectual

Human in Person

dynamics in a social and institutional context is immeasurably difficult. But why else would one want to be a vice-chancellor?

1. Am I proud of having been the Vice-chancellor?

2. Was it worth all that I was forced to go through?

I had given everything of myself to make Bangalore University a university with potential for excellence. BU has offered me no grace or peace. BU for the last several months has romanticised agitation and celebrated chaos. Protests have been engineered. An atmosphere of intolerance was spread across the campus.

There should have been an honest engagement on differences repositioning BU from being hypercritical to being factual. I have worked towards lifting the University from the slime and sludge and corrupted mind set.

I gave my best to the silent majority of students and faculty in BU in the form of well founded reforms in exam division, academic and administration. Because of the silence of the Silent Majority everything went unsung and unnoticed.

It is sad that outstanding achievements like the 9th place amongst 560 Universities in India went flushed in the toilets of BU hostels.

Bangalore school of Economics was sabotaged. Plans to start schools of communication, Commerce and Law in tune with National Law School and converting The University Vishweshvariah College of engineering into an IIT went for a toss.

The Fight was between silent majority and a hand full of loud and outrageous interests. As the vested interests were loud as they hogged the show and achievements were buried in the cacophony of the few.

The journey as vice chancellor.

My years as Vice-chancellor of BU are a paradox.

It was a dance that i was made to walk; It was a song I was made to speak and a laugh that I was made to choke. Well -One who laughs last- laughs best?

It was sad to see the crumbling walls of reforms right in front of my eyes even before I had put in my papers.

I have put in place a social responsibility for the university in transmission of knowledge, thought and values over these three years. While planning the future I have looked at higher education wherein costs were not looked at as expenditure but as a social investment. The basic truth about life is that it moves on and nothing is immune to the effects of time.The primitive instincts have triumphed!

The media has been by and large insensitive to the hurt and pain it has caused to me personally. They have never given any credit for the path breaking reforms introduced in the university. That's fine with me. That's the media mind set. For you in the media -Good news is bad news, Bad news is good and the worst is the best.

My mission was to make a positive difference in the career and lives of Bangalore University Students and the faculty. On a day such as this one I am proud of what the university has achieved over its Sixty four years of existence; reflect on the sacrifices of those before us and indeed reaffirm the dedication to the pursuant of the noble mission that constitutes the cornerstone of the existence of this cherished university.

A borderless society with no divisions of caste and community can only arise, from borderless minds. Love, patience, good laws and fair justice are the best instruments for our society to transform itself into a borderless community where hands that serve are better than lips that pray.As I retrospect the three and a half years of my tenure as a Vice Chancellor, I am fond of Charles Dickens's famous Utterances, "It was the best of times; it was the worst of times.

Deva U are 64+

Deva you are not alone. There are 650 million in this world. 2 billion people will be aged 60 and older by 2050. This represents both challenges and opportunities. The world population is rapidly ageing.

There are 1000-year old trees in the mountain, but not many 100 year-old people"At the most, you live until 100 years old (only 1 in 100,000). If you live until 90, you only have 30 years. If you live until 80, you only have 20 years.

I Do not worry about what will happen after I am gone, because when I return to dust, I will feel nothing about praises or criticisms. Don't expect too much from your children. Don't trade in your health for wealth anymore because your money may not be able to buy your health.

Between 2000 and 2050, the proportion of the world's population over 60 years will double from about 11% to 22%. The absolute number of people aged 60 years and over is expected to increase from 605 million to 2 billion over the same period. The world will have more people who live to see their 80s or 90s than ever before.

The number of people aged 80 years or older, for example, will have almost quadrupled to 395 million between 2000 and 2050.

I have heard of the three ages of man - youth, middle age, and still -you're looking wonderful- age. I have grown old too soon and smart too late- Sixty Five something. I am not too sure where I am!

I turned sixty-five in September. Wow! I got here a lot faster than I would have ever imagined possible. Well they say seventy is the new forty," Is Sixty- The New Thirty? I am 65 and something and feel young. When I look in the mirror I keep wondering who that "old" person is -looking at me!!!.

Whenever I hear the words, "How old are you," I stutter for an answer: My chronological age is a matter of years in existence, my biological age is vital, my psychological age is growing, my emotional age is mature and my functional age is young.

As I am getting at 65 yrs I feel that days are too short and am surprised that it is only 24 hrs that make a day. Why an odd figure like 24 hrs ? why was it not rounded off to say 25. What is the compelling reason that a day has to be only 24 hrs? Hard to believe that back in the eighties I was the thirty and something and I felt I had the world by the tail. May be i should have felt that i held it by the horns!

I get up every day vibrant and highly positive. We are capable of so much more now. Think about it. We have so much experience in life. people have worked many years doing different things that probably did not excite them, but which they felt was necessary to provide a standard of living for their families and themselves. Yes one has to live for others too.

My vision is to get people over age 65 reignited in their life. Change your mindset and start thinking about what is new for you, what can you experience next, how you can do it. I believe –The Best is yet to be. Actually, I have always believed that the best is yet to be. It is a very positive attitude in engaging life.

I consider myself a life-long learner. I find it exhilarating to learn new stuff! I believe that everything we do in our lives helps to formulate everything we accomplish. I have lived my life with various philosophies from early on. One of them is to accept every decision I've made as a learning experience. We all do things that we can look back on and feel some regret. But never regret anything that made you smile once.

Do it or do not do it — you will regret both." Never have any regret for the past and never have any fear of the future. I abhor intolerance, it solves nothing. But how does that serve us? Is it not better to look back on our life decisions and remember that we made them with the best intentions and best knowledge we had at the time?

Well, I have been hurt in my life. Indeed Quite a bit. No one goes through life unscathed. Refuse to define your life by any single event, whatever it may be even if it is a real part of your life but that is – just a part. Storms produce strength and character. I dislike hard times but in looking back over my life I can see that the hard times have made me who I am today. I am a flawed man. If I deny this painful truth I condemn myself to a life of secrecy and deception. Life is too short to hold a grudge. In every situation I can be part of the problem or I can be part of the solution. The choice is mine and yours too.

Aging is something that kind of sneaks up on you. One moment you are 30 and all of a sudden you're 65 something.. How did that happen? Aging gracefully means accepting the changes in your outward appearance and focusing on others instead of yourself. Tell the people in your life how much you love them and do it often. Communication is an art. Don't take life for granted. Count your blessings and thank God for them.

I have learned to laugh at myself and not take things too seriously, what can otherwise be taken lightly. Learn to smile when you are hurt. Don't take the smile off even when life is hard and troubled. when asked about your age- don't hesitate to tell a lie. No you are not committing a fraud. It's tempting. I can still pass off for a lot younger than the ordinary stereotype of sixty five +.

If I am having a bad hair day, it is OK. I am thankful I still have some hair for dyeing. Heartaches and stresses are in plenty but easier to handle because of my life experiences. When I was younger, I was optimistic. As a sixty-something where do i stand? still optimistic and more realistic. I'm feeling it is curiosity and excitement about things on hand.

I am comfortable with excellence. I am angry and bored with mediocrity. Nothing has changed and the repetition is mind numbing. The people who make a difference in your life are not the ones with the most credentials, the most money, or the most awards but the ones that care who make the impact.

With age i have become more merciful and less critical towards myself. I have become my best friend! As the years go by it's easier to stay positive. I care less for what others think of me. I have stopped doubting myself. I have earned the right to make mistakes and due course corrections as I deem it fit!I go to the beach and roam in my shorts and the paunch much to the pity of the onlookers. I don't care because I know that they too will get old.

I know that I forget sometimes. That is fine as long as I remember all the right things. I cannot think of being an Alzimer.. I have sufferd heart breaks. But broaken hearts give us the strength understanding and compassion. An Unbroken heart is hard and callous. It cannot understand the joy of imperfection.

Now my hairs what ever is left with have turned grey. But still old is old. I am satisfied feeling young while getting along with my biological age. I don't very much like the mirror and the one shown to me .I am content. I am practicing to keep my smile for ever. I have lost some very special people in my life- My Parents and My elder sister. I have prayed for peace to accept the loss and thank God for having brought them into my life. Their memories are written on my heart and etched in the brain and mind. I hope he is keeping them with him!

I have decided to enjoy my life while I am still on this earth. I try to have a good attitude because it makes me nicer. Aging gracefully is a choice. You can crib a lot about the lost opportunities, lack of comfort and short of finances. Does it change anything? I don't know how long it will last or if the details will be remembered, but I hope to enjoy the trip. I believe in a fresh start every morning. I greet god every morning with hope and pleasure. I always think as to make the day simple for me and others. I pray god not to complicate anything for me. I carry the contentment of a good night sleep and a clean heart. I pray to him that there should not be any issue that He and I together cannot solve!

I have learnt over the years not to focus on hurt and betrayals. I am not a slave of the routine. I prefer to have a long walk early in the morning amidst greenery and quietness. I try to meditate. Prayer is when you talk to god. Meditation is when you listen to god.

I truly believe that we look "like" what we eat. When we eat raw fruits, vegetables and other wholesome foods on a daily basis we'll have more energy, our skin begins to clear and reveals a natural glow, and it doesn't matter what age we are! Try it for two weeks and see for yourself. We all know, the most important aspect of having nice clear skin is eating fresh fruits and vegetables daily. If you can take an extra fifteen minutes in the morning to juice some carrots, apples, pears, etc in the blender each morning, or even every other day, you will notice a skin improvement within weeks. The natural foods in life are what work best.

We have been blessed with everything we need to stay healthy and wise. And yet, many of us do not take heed to this important part of life that has been freely given to us. We believe the miracle to wrinkles is found in a bottle. We tend to make our health and other important aspects of our life, harder than it should be. But eating for good health is so simple and readily available.

'

I'm finding out that there is no such thing as "retirement". There is youthful service, no matter the age. There is the joy of major leaps and small gains; there is no such thing as "age-appropriate" behavior. Shop until you drop? No. It's serve until you drop, sliding into home plate, glad and full of love, ready to find out what's next. Stay excited about each day. Its treasure what you've got.

Do I have any regrets? Yes a few! I wish I had been less of myself. I wish I had been a better human and a better friend .I wish I was a better son, a better father, a better doctor and so on, The list is endless. At the end of your life, the only regrets will not be the things you did… it will be the things you didn't do. Is it too late to start doing things have not done, yet i always wanted to! It's never too late. If you have not talked to your neighbour for some unfriendly event forget and forgive and go and speak to them and tell them that you missed them and that you are sorry. And things like that". The worst thing about regret is that it sneaks up on you.

Life is fun and exciting and I am grateful to be here to say that. We are so very fortunate to be alive at this time in our country in general. But, think about it. We are in the best country in the world. With the technology we have access to what a wonderful time to be alive! But for now let's be joyful for the way we look and feel, and take care of ourselves the best we can.

My Sunday mornings will remain, of taking a healthy walk or turning great music on the stereo, I'll be sipping coffee from my armchair, waiting for common sense to erupt from the idiot box- -one definition of insanity.

I have the luxury of a sixty something, not audacious but still hopeful. It was only last week when it hit me that I'm a sexagenarian, a person between the ages of 60 and 70. The term made me laugh. I wonder: what do they call people in their fifties? I'll tell you when I find out. Old age is fifteen years older than I am. I was wrong to grow older, Pity. I was happy in my youth. I am responsible now.

To be seventy years young is far more cheerful and hopeful than to be forty years old. The years between fifty and seventy are the hardest. You are always being asked to do more, and you are not yet decrepit enough to turn them down. People tell you that you are too old to do a job only to get that done from you! Don't fall a prey for that. Do only what is to be done and if you are comfortable1

Old wood is best to burn, old wine to drink, old friends to trust, and old authors to read. AND always remember life is not measured by the number of breaths we take, but by the moments that take our breath away!" "Millions saw the apple fall, but only Newton asked why."

THERE is no magic pill for staying youthful. It may be hard to swallow if you're looking for a quick fix but the answer is regular exercise and a consistently healthy diet. I recently became a grandfather.. This was a joyous event in our family, and my first emotion was indeed joy -- for the new parents, for the healthy boy. But I confess that my second reaction -- and not far behind -- was much more conflicted: I'm too young to be a grandfather, I found myself thinking-Don't grandparents drive slowly?

My Grandchild did not make me feel old; it's the knowledge that I am married to a grandmother does!- Within weeks I found myself upping my cardio routine and modifying my diet a bit, with the idea of shedding a couple of pounds. I eat with Heart in Mind.

I should do more sit-ups, too. But i realise that the knees hurt. Who knows, maybe I'll even train for a walkathon. Hell no: If you act old, you'll feel old. Don't accept the stereotypes of the elderly as debilitated, out to pasture. Many men lose hair as they age, so that balding -- like gray hair and wrinkles -- is a common and potent trigger for an aging mindset.

You are as young as your faith, as old as your doubt; as young as your self- confidence, as old as your fear; as young as your hope, as old as your despair. Growing old is mandatory; growing up is optional.

You are old when you forget names, then you forget faces, then you forget to pull your zipper up, then you forget to pull your zipper down.

In youth the days are short and the years are long; in old age the years are short and the days long. The years have taught me much which the days never knew. Inflation is when you pay fifteen dollars for the ten-dollar haircut you used to get for five dollars when you had hair. I have always wondered How old would i be if I didn't know how old I am? Forty is the old age of youth; fifty the youth of old age. ~Victor Hugo

The first half of life consists of the capacity to enjoy without the chance; the last half consists of the chance without the capacity. ~Mark Twain

"Age is an issue of mind over matter. If you don't mind, it doesn't matter."

- Mark Twain

People who claim that higher knowledge will free us from suffering are fooling themselves. But to do so to the point of obsession only invites another form of pride. I have a friend who has given up drinking alcohol.,cigarettes, coffee, eggs, meat, milk. He eats oat bran for breakfast, takes mega doses of vitamins C and E, rides his Exercise Bicycle religiously, and never uses his microwave oven. He may not live any longer than his least prudent neighbor, but as his physician told him, it will certainly seem longer! A Whole Other Stage" begins with the line "I've reached the stage where my lawyer, my broker, my allergies, and my CA are all significantly younger than I am.

So I have begun already to do some of the things I hope to spend more time doing during my eventual retirement-Professional or otherwise I find that they are not as fulfilling as I had hoped, I still have time to make some course corrections. "Don't put off until tomorrow the things you can do today and it is good if clichéd advice".

One of the good things that I have found as I grow older is how much closer to the surface my emotions have become. My sense of empathy, of feeling with others, has grown stronger with time. How can people get older and meaner? Can someone please explain that to me? That is something I guess I will never get. Life seems more precious to me these days.

Youth," someone has said, "is wasted on the young." Of course, it's not completely correct, and it has the smell of bitterness or envy about it. I really don't think I would want to go back. Life is richer now that I have traveled sixty five years along its path, and I would not give that up. As the great artist Pablo Picasso once said, "It takes a long time to become young."

Prayer as We Grow Older which each of us does with every tick of the clock-

With all this 60+ is a great time to be alive. At times I seem a bit overwhelmed. For me personally, I can get mesmerized checking out stuff online. Face book is one thing I don't get into too often. There is so much information available to us about anything-That is if we know how to access it.

Many people feel unhappy, health-wise and security-wise, after 60 years of age owing to the diminishing importance given to them and their opinion. Never say 'I am aged'. Health is wealth- Preserve your health. Do take health insurance cover and not be a burden on anybody for any eventuality.

You're Never Too Old to Do Something Amazing. What you want from life understands that what you do right now drives your future.

Money is important:

When I was young I thought that money was the most important thing in life now that I am old I know that it is.

There are two things that I can definitely confess about money in my life, personally.

1. I cannot survive without it.

2. It does not control me.

Money is only important when you don't have enough of it. It is easy to think "If only I had more money" all my problems would be solved. Yes I agree to some extent. When you have excess money then your set of problems becomes different. The new problems can be a lot harder for you to manage than the simple lack of money was. Your life suddenly becomes more complicated rather than free of problems. When you have too much money you can't blame your problems on lack of money. The only answer that remains is you must blame yourself for your lack of happiness.

"Money can't buy happiness, but it can make the search a lot more comfortable". I forget who first said that, but it's a fact.. Money, at the very least, relieves one of the daily stresses of worrying about money, something most people do, most of the time.

Having money isn't enough. It's how you value it, use it, grow it, and spend it, that matter most. People often run after money because they get addicted to the idea of accumulating money.

A popular greeting card attributes this quote to Henry David Thoreau: Happiness is like a butterfly: the more you chase it, the more it will elude you. But if you turn your attention to other things, it will come and sit softly on you. Don't Worry, Be Happy.

Remember, Money Can't Buy Happiness

Research shows that once income climbs above the poverty level, more money brings very little extra happiness. Relentless pursuit of happiness itself is futile. It's never going to bring about an enduring state of happiness. Foster Friendship! There are few better antidotes to unhappiness than close friendships with people who care about you.

Use it right, and money becomes positive power to transform the world. It's how it's used that determines its value and usefulness.

Money can't buy me love, the Beatles once sang. But no one has tried buying it without money! Can you spend Your Way to Happiness? No, money does not play a negative role! It is a fact that wealthy people have better health and medical care, more meaningful work, and extra free time. If you are not happy spending money it is possible that you are not spending it right!

In these lean times, it's smart to be frugal.. You can maintain your health even though you cannot rule your health. Money helps you with that. A lot of people globally postpone health checkups because they don't have enough money to pay for health care bills. Again money's role in health maintenance is irrefutable.

Money is an aphrodisiac.

Who does not need money? The powerful to the weak, A sage to a monk, a mortal to an immortal, an ordinary to the extra ordinary- everyone needs money. Human beings are the only species of all gods creations who need money. There have been wars to acquire, to hold on to and to enhabce the quantum of money. The countries in the world are classified as economically rich and poor. You need money, I need money and every one does!

You need money for the basic necessities of life, for your and family's health, for education, for upbringing etc. If you have amassed wealth you earn the unqualified respect from the society and the community. If you have no money, if you are dependent on someone you are treated like dust and as a waste body. The respect you earn is directly proportional to the money you have.

You need money for the basic necessities of life, for your and family's health, for education, for upbringing etc. If you have amassed wealth you earn the unqualified respect from the society and the community. If you have no money, if you are dependent on someone you are treated like dust and as a waste body. The respect you earn is directly proportional to the money you have.

The first question that merits an answer is what makes an individual smart? It is the wisdom to make a sound decision at the crucial moment, or knowing how to make the best out of the bad situation. They don't feel defeated just because they need to revaluate their beliefs. They don't permit their past to hold them back. They don't rely on good luck to solve their problems. They don't hesitate to learn from their and others mistakes. They don't overestimate their abilities. They tell only facts..

Don't spend beyond your means even for yourkids. You have lived for them all through and it is time you enjoyed a harmonious life with yourwife / husband. If your kids remain grateful and they take care of you, you are blessed. But never take it for granted. Relaxation and recreation is essential- if possible with the family and if not, all by yourself. Live this moment. This is enlightened selfishness.

Forget and forgive:

It is often said that a person is the sum of their memories. Your memory and recall is what makes you who you are. Is there a loss of memory that is stored in the brain? it is said that memory is difficult to access if the event or person is far away and appears too far in between. It is not the memory but what goes off is the ability to retrieve it!

In the real world you'd have to build in some system for discounting old, useless info. In fact, of course, we all have one of these super-brains with a discounting system: we call it 'forgetting'. But it is also true that once you have learnt swimming you are a swimmer for life though the gap may be considerably long.

All of us have memories we'd prefer to forget, that foot-in-the-mouth moment. Quashing memories could impede our recall. To remember a piece of information, the person would need to be aware of it in the first place. We tend to have troubles with time especially for things like dates and times that are a moving target, constantly in flux. So, unless I have a calendar in front of me, or have reason to check it on my phone, it tends to slip away.

As we come to learn more about memory, I hope that researchers will dig more deeply into the emotional and social impacts of differences in memory.

Whenever angry feelings about a person who's harmed you enter your mind, tell yourself: "We are all good, loving souls who occasionally get lost." Pray for this person to find their way back to a happier place. Well this too much! When you are tempted to focus on all the ways the world has done you wrong, instead count your blessings.

Bury the hatchet. Let bygones be bygones. The grudge stops here. For much of human history, forgiveness has been a religious concept. Today scientists tend to agree that holding a serious grudge can cause stress, which has a toxic effect on your body.

Unforgiveness—defined as repeatedly thinking about an injustice you've suffered through a lens of vengeance, hostility, bitterness, resentment, anger, sadness, or all of the above—can raise your blood pressure and can be lethal. But is forgiveness the only—or best—way to purge you of unforgiveness? No, says Worthington. Here is a mindbender: Successful settling of scores will also do the trick. Part of the reason that forgiving is so difficult may be that getting back and returning the insult or injury feels so good. it can be a powerful form of self-protection self preservation. It is a natural way of protecting ourselves, does forgiveness make us weak? No, Forgiveness is equally innate—and an adaptation that also improves our odds of survival.

Forgiving a good friend who has apologized for hurting you makes a lot of sense. Unconditional forgiveness is a bit of a misnomer:

Forgiveness purports to wash away the hurts completely. How Can I Forgive You? This torments quit a few who are unrepentant of the hurt they have caused. One should have the courage to forgive retaining the freedom not to forget.

Don't be bothered too much about others' mistakes. Be not spiritual enough to show other cheek when you are slapped on one. Accept yourself as you are and also accept others for what they are. Everybody is unique and right in his/ their own way. Accept dying and overcome the fear of end. Yes you cannot overcome the end but certainly don't live in fear of the impending death.The most fascinating aspect of human life is that everyone knows that everyone dies. While you are alive you always think that death happens to others and not to you. It is a nice feeling that you are immortal till you die.

We think that our children and wives and kith and kin will be unable to withstand our loss. But the truth is no one is going to die for you; they may be depressed for some time. Time heals everything and they will carry on. Life insurance, at this point, can benefit not only you, but your family most especially. Just think what great a burden can be taken off from their shoulders when you have arranged for the payment of all the bills all expenses are taken care of. By this, you will be able to help them adjust smoothly to your departure. Moreover, when you have life insurance at 60, you can also use this to leave something behind not only for your kids, but for your grand kids as well.

Attitude of Gratitude

A growing body of research suggests that maintaining an attitude of gratitude can improve psychological, emotional and physical well-being. It turns out; giving thanks is good for your health.

They're also less likely to be depressed, envious, greedy or alcoholics.

Gratitude as an indispensable human virtue, but social scientists are beginning to study how it develops and the effects it can have. Counting blessings can actually make people feel better. Gratitude is actually a demanding, complex emotion that requires "self-reflection and the humility to realize one's own limitations. Delivering your thanks in person can be particularly powerful.

Even you can refuse with a polite 'No Thanks". When people are given freedom to choose, they will take it as their right

Can Gratitude be a Gimmick? More than ever before we are being called,, to embrace an "attitude of gratitude." Gratitude is something everyone likes. No one is anti-gratitude. It is said that show of extreme humility is a sign of an ulterior motive. Be watchful. I believe gratitude is a good, even necessary practice. But maybe some expressions of gratitude have a shallow side. Maybe gratitude isn't good when it's a gimmick.

I always long for expressions of appreciation, perhaps even more so when they are not expected. Seemingly small gestures of gratitude and kindness enrich our lives and the lives of others. A Serving of Gratitude May save the Day for you as a stitch in time saves nine! The power of gratitude is the emotion of friendship. Think of even one note of thanks you might write or one act of kindness you might undertake that may be the first step towards a blossoming of hope.

Attitude is an expression of favor or disfavour toward a person, place, thing, or event. Attitude can be formed from a person's past and present. Problem is not the Problem. Problem is your bad attitude.

ABC model of attitudes: A for affective, B for behavioral, and C for cognitive. Although every attitude has these three components, any particular attitude can be based on one component more than another.

I have decided to stick with love. Hatred is too great a burden to bear.

- Martin Luther King, Jr.

When one door of happiness closes, another opens; but often we look so long at the closed door that we do not see the one which has been opened for us.

- Helen Keller

The Power of Positive Attitude Can Change Your Life. I believe Happiness is a Choice and I could choose to be happy.

Negativity attracts Negative people and you will be influenced by their thoughts. There is the positive aspect in everything, in every person and in every situation. A more positive attitude, I realized I had to reinforce these thoughts and behaviours in myself. Be positive with others. be nice, be kind, be helpful, be gentle, Listen to them.

A stream of self-help gurus have spent time on Oprah's stage over the past decade and a half, all with the same message. You have choices in life. External conditions don't determine your life. You do. It's all inside you, in your head, in your wishes and desires. Thoughts are destiny, so thinking positive thoughts will enable positive things to happen.

Cultivate Gratitude

Gratitude shifts people away from bitterness and despair, and promotes happiness. Holding a grudge and nursing grievances can affect physical and emotional health. Finally, try to hold on to the forgiveness. Don't dwell on your anger, hurt, and desire for vengeance.

Foster Forgiveness- This reduces the power of bad events to create bitterness and resentment,

God gave you a gift of 86,400 seconds today. Have you used one to say 'thank you?' Yes I have! I thank god for everything every day. Yes I pray to show my gratitude to Him.I pray to god to keep me healthy, wealthy and prevent difficulties and accidents and to keep me in a state of contentment.

For each new morning with its light,

For rest and shelter of the night,

For health and food, for love and friends,

For everything–Thank you god!

Gratitude is the best attitude. Gratitude is the most exquisite form of courtesy. Through sickness we recognize the value of health; through evil, the value of good; through hunger, the value of food; through exertion, the value of rest.

While eating bamboo sprouts, remember the man who planted them. Be content with what you have received; be thankful for what you have escaped. Reflect upon your present blessings, of which every man has plenty; not on your misfortunes of which all men have some.

Every language in the world has a way of saying "thank you." This is because gratitude is an inherent quality that resides within each human being, and is triggered and expressed spontaneously in a variety of different contexts. Gratitude crosses all boundaries—creed, age, vocation, gender, and nation—and is emphasized by all the great religious traditions.

Gratitude unlocks and enhances the fullness of life. It turns what we have into enough and more. It turns denial into acceptance, chaos to order, confusion to clarity. It can turn a meal into a feast, a house into a home, a stranger into a friend.

Gratitude is not only the greatest of the virtues, but the parent of all of the others – Cicero (106–43bc)

Gratitude is shown in acts. We learned about gratitude and humility that so many people had a hand in our success from the teachers who inspired us to the janitors who kept our school clean. Gratitude is a feeling that spontaneously emerges from within. However, it is not simply an emotional response; it is also a choice we make.

Virtues are qualities that support the inherent goodness that resides within each human being. Gratitude is a virtue. I am grateful for all the simple blessings I've taken for granted. Yes our society is adept at making us keenly aware of the things we don't have. We're always seeking something better. We can't help it. Our perspective quickly becomes warped. In our never ending chase for the good life we find ourselves trapped on the work-to-spend treadmill, stressed with jobs we dislike

Yes, being born here we've hit the jackpot – but we're too busy chasing bigger and better riches and comforts. We take so much for granted. Billions of people around the world, would trade places with us in a second. The first step to financial freedom is developing an attitude of gratitude. It's liberating to focus on what we do have, instead of dwelling on what we don't – to realize how lucky we are in the grand scheme of things. Compared to the rest of the world we are already living the good life.

Welcome every morning with a smile-Another golden opportunity to complete what you were unable to finish yesterday Today will never happen again. No better words than thank you have yet been discovered to express the sincere gratitude of one's heart; when the two words are sincerely spoken. Stop and take a moment to admire all the beautiful things you take for granted every day,

Someone is enjoying shade today because someone planted a tree a long time ago." ~ Warren Buffett.

A Bad Attitude Is Like A Flat Tyre, You Can't Go Anywhere Until You Change It. I read this quote from somewhere and it really stuck to me. Approaching things with a good and positive attitude will get you places in life. I know all of us have great qualities, and we have to learn to utilize them and show them to the world. Go with the flow and never be afraid to swim against the flow if required. Yes it is the dead fish that go with the flow.

The good side about attitude is that you are not born with it, you just can change and shape it until it fits best with your desired goals. A good attitude toward everything around you is more efficient. As they say, the attitude is everything. It's free and it can only produce good outcome, so keep an open mind and a powerfully grateful attitude!

He does things daily for me; I do things daily for him. That's how relationships work, give and take. Even if it's routine, never take it for granted. So, a simple 'thank you' and tight hug does wonders, no matter how many times it happens! Hand writing your feelings are such a strong way to show appreciation and gratitude.

Even if you have to disagree do so with gratitude. Always listen to the other person with empathy and compassion. Don't be afraid to share how you feel, no matter how vulnerable! Ninety-nine percent of the time we have an opportunity to be grateful for something. We just don't notice it. We go through our days in a daze.

Eternity is not a long, long time. Eternity is the opposite of time. It is no time. How can we free ourselves from chronological time to live in eternal time? Character

Character is the root of the tree; conduct is the fruit it bears.

Character is what you are! Conduct is what you do.

The mental and ethical qualities distinctive to an individual **Is** the character of that person? Our Character Is What Determines How We Respond to the Situations and Circumstances of Life

We all fall into the trap of judging a person's character by their appearance. How wrong we are! All too often, the real character of the person only appears when some negative event hits them or you. Then you may see a toxic person emerging from and it is often a shock. Determining a person's real character can be a difficult feat.

The best index to a person's character is how he treats people who can't do him any good, and how he treats people who can't fight back. Kindness is the hall mark of a person with a good character. Be honest and trustworthy. Have good values. Never compromise your values. Be a good friend, wife or husband and family member. Be loyal! Stand tall, chin up and smile. Be courageous and strong. Make a positive internal commitment to you, family, friends, to constant learning, work, nature, and other worthwhile causes. Reward yourself and Dream of success. Live your dreams. Be enthusiastic.

Conduct is the outward life. Character is the life unseen, hidden within, yet evidenced by that which is seen. Conduct is external, seen from without; character is internal -- operating within. Character and conduct are integral to faith. One cannot exist without the other.

Words are a powerful tool that we have at our disposal every waking moment. We can create a strong mindset by consistently thinking positive thoughts. Take the blame for the faults from you. Be modest about your achievements and show humility. Shower appreciation on others, Show empathy towards poor and the disabled. One can acquire everything in solitude, except character.

The smallest decisions I make during my day say a lot about me. Where I choose to spend my money, how I choose to spend my time, if I bend over and pick up a piece of garbage or walk right past it, the conversation I hold with the grocery store clerk — each of these things gives me valuable information about myself if I'm willing to pay attention to it.

Create the habits by replacing words and thoughts: For all I know teenagers are a hard nut to crack when it comes to controlling their activities and behaviors. Parents need to be tactful in handling the needs of their kids in Teenage. Always listen first and communicate effectively.

To begin with the parent should not reciprocate the anger. Never assume your teens to be wrong. Teach them what's right and wrong. Build trust. Stop being over- protective parent. The difference that makes one flourish, cherish, and perish is a person's attitude. Attitude cannot be thrust upon anybody. It is a self-nourishing ingredient that an individual should possess.

A word of caution – don't go overboard by becoming a noisy cheerleader who spends more effort on projecting your attitude than nurturing it. Above all, don't try to be someone you are not! Be who you are… Project the real thing! Be authentic!

Life is a learning journey and all we can do is to strive to do our best each day.

The poverty

Don't just get Outraged by India's poverty estimates, understand them!

Poverty is the inability of getting choices and opportunities, loss of human dignity. Malnourishment and impoverished, uneducated, unhealthy and unemployed is it possible to live with dignity? No access to credit. Vulnerable to riots and susceptible to infections living in slums and inhabitable conditions with no access to even drinking water! One third of deaths – some 18 million people a year or 50,000 per day – are due to poverty-related causes.

How the Poor Live? No they don't .They merely survive; every other day is a bonus.

From Eleventh National Development Plan

50% of Indians do not have proper shelter; 70% do not have access to decent toilets, 85% of villages don't have a secondary school, Over 40% of these same villages don't have proper roads -

Can anyone really live on Rs. 26 a day, the income of the officially poor in rural India? India's Mean National Income was Rs. 4,500 a month, or Rs. 150 a day. People spend about a third of their incomes on rent. Excluding rent, they have Rs. 100 each a day.. Seventy-five per cent Indians live on less than this average.

Why there is so much disparity? Are the 75% of the people earning less than the average less deserving to earn a decent livelihood?Every year 40% of the Indian population go below the poverty line because of out of pocket expences on health related issues. We don't know the answers to these questions. We are not even feeling for the huge gulf between the haves and have-nots.

I think we have failed as a society. The have-nots do not has any alternatives other than staying hungry. if they fall sick they have no insurance and they have no money. May be it is cheaper to die!. It is so disgusting. The only way forward is to create a society where people will get equal opportunities.

Spiritual beliefs.

I am Spiritual but not religious."

Although the terms are often used interchangeably, they have different meanings. Religion is a specific set of organized beliefs and practices, usually shared by a group. Spirituality is more individual, and has to do with a sense of peace, purpose, and connection to others, and beliefs about the meaning of life.

My spiritual beliefs are more personalized, less structured, more open to new ideas/influences, and more pluralistic than those of the doctrinal faiths of organized religions. For me spirituality includes introspection and the development of an individual's inner life through practices such as meditation, prayer and contemplation. I understood spirituality as the search for or the development of inner peace and the foundations of happiness. The spiritual practice of some kind is essential for personal well being.

Spirituality is positive psychology. Spirituality is not possible without strict adherence to peace and respect for the other. Compassion is the bedrock of human life. When you were born, you had no beliefs. As one grows one learnt things and formed beliefs. So, what is a belief? It is the building block we use to create our experience of life itself, and it is the key to what kind of life we live.

Three passions have governed my life: The longings for love, the search for knowledge, and compassion for the suffering of mankind. I have wanted to understand the Hearts of people. I have sought knowledge with passion. But always compassion has brought me back to earth; Cries of pain reverberated in my heart -Of hungry kids, of tortured innocents and of old people left helpless and homeless.

I have no patience for any religion that wants to force into my private life. God has sent so many down here to "save our souls". Why do they offer such contrary teachings? Is God as contradictory as his "messengers" make him appear? If God truly wants us to learn about him, why does he send along such mixed messages?

we are the most destructive form of life on this planet- Look at the love for guns and wars after we declared ourselves "civilized". Witness the tears of the small kids hungry and scared, waiting for the return of parents not living anymore. There are lots of things about God that I don't understand. I don't understand why he created man even though he knew ahead of time what we would be like.

I long to alleviate the evil but I cannot. Why give people chance after chance after chance? Why not punish the evil right here and now. Punishment will come all too soon for many people for wrongs committed sooner than later. As I said I don't understand why God is the way he is. I'm glad that he did create us and that he did give us free choice. The motivation, the intent and the emotion behind our thought, words and actions, as I've just said all of the beautiful words in the world will come to zero if in your heart you are full of fear .

Understanding of God.

Tears are a Language God understands .But why the god waits till you breakdown? Do we understand him?

God as the sum total of all the Laws, and all the energies governed by these Laws which make up everything in the manifested and un-manifested universe — all that we see and cannot see. God is also the great Cosmic being who encircles this planet. Man, in turn, is a 'Spark of God, expressing itself through a physical body. Each one of us is essentially divine but, demonstrates this divinity only to a limited degree.

You found God? If nobody claims him in thirty days, he's yours!

—Author unknown

Spiritual belief is like a mirror. No theories, no ideas, no history, no science. Just a mirror that reflects all that we were, we are— and we will be. I cannot tell you what this mirror shows to you, for that is for you to see and decide. Does it show you God? Does it show you Man? Does it show you nothing? Or does it show you everything?

I doubt my doubts and believe my beliefs.

My understanding of God includes omniscience, omnipotence, Omnipresence, perfect goodness and divine simplicity. God exists objectively and independently in human thought. That God creates and sustains everything. That God is omnipotent and interacts with the universe through prayers and meditation. The God is more complex than simply being the sum total of the universe.

God is that invisible power. Everyone knows that god does exist. God is understood by many different names, such as God, Spirit, Supreme Being, Intelligence, Mind, Energy, Nature and so forth.

He is also believed to be transcendent meaning that God is outside space and time. Therefore, God is eternal and unable to be changed by earthly forces or anything else within its creation.

God is Absolute .It is the concept of an unconditional reality. God to me evokes a whole lot of feelings. He invokes love. He invokes Fear. God loves as a doting parent. We have to earn God's love through our suffering and pain. God is a punisher. There is an overwhelming tide of people who are god fearing than god loving on this earth.

We fear God's punishment. God is rewarding and encouraging. We feel safe. The more love we give the more we have. God is fear;

God is judging and evaluating. God is accepting and forgiving. God is powerful. We feel in constant communication with a Higher Power that supports and strengthens us. A person's sin is the reason for divine rejection and punishment.

God is a difficult concept to those who choose not to believe. I can't prove God. I can't disprove God. Regardless of their orientation, most believe that god exists without evidence. I would add -God...by definition is that he is beyond man's power to conceive.

WHAT'S UP, GOD?

If God did not exist, it would be necessary to invent Him.

—Voltaire

A witty saying proves nothing. I agree.

I believe it's all Ego. How can I possibly non-exist.? God serves an indispensable function in the public sphere.

The notion of God is deeply entrenched in the collective consciousness of the human race The primary role played by God in society is that of an authority figure.

The fear of God and divine justice kept all of society "scared straight" for a long time. Today, we are still influenced by our fear of God's wrath. No matter if he is called Luck or Fate or Entropy, God is the line we all compulsively toe. The question of his existence is there

If i am inevitable and if i do not exist i should be invented as i am indispensable. God is inevitable so he better exist or else He is to be invented. One who lives by sword dies by the sword. So a sword has to be invented and created.

Some say there is a God; others say there is no God. The truth probably lies somewhere in between. Let us understand- First things first. Why do we need to search for God? We all know that- god is somewhere taking care of things. The believers have their belief, the atheists their disbelief, and the agnostics their ambivalence. Then why bother?

Is god not eternal? There are no cycles of birth or rebirth for Him. If there is no god there would total chaos. How do the precise laws of gravity and motion work and how are they regulated? If god has to be created, who creates Him? Is He going to be as powerful? Any answers?

Bernard Shaw knew that men must have religion with god as its chief! o did Fritz Schumacher, Of Small is Beautiful fame. God is our understanding of an All-Perfect Being, good and noble. God- is ultimately responsible for the character of the natural world.

The origin and nature of our Universe points towards God's existence in many ways Hinduism, Buddhism, Jainism and Sikhism were all born in India. But none of them legally exist in India as a state religion. The only Hindu state in the world -The country of Nepal has also become a secular state.

Unity in diversity is the slogan before us. Tolerance towards each other is integrated in the constitution.

Buddhists do not worship any gods or God. People outside of Buddhism often think that Buddhists worship the Buddha. However, the Buddha -Siddhartha Gautama never claimed to be divine, but rather he is viewed by Buddhists as having attained what they are also striving to attain, which is spiritual enlightenment and, with it, freedom from the continuous cycle of life and rebirth.

Muslims believe there is one almighty God, named Allah, who is infinitely superior to and transcendent from humankind. Allah is viewed as the creator of the universe. Everything that happens is Allah's will. He is powerful and strict, who will be merciful toward followers depending on the sufficiency of their life's good works and religious devotion. A follower's relationship with Allah is as a servant to Allah.

Jesus Christ as a teacher of enlightenment performed miracles, forgave people of their sin and said that anyone who believed in him would have eternal life. Spirituality is not religion and is not even necessarily affiliated with religion.

Those who see themselves as "spiritual, but not religious" reject traditional organized religion as the sole-or even the most valuable-means of furthering their spiritual growth. Spirituality exists wherever we struggle with the issue of how our lives fit into the greater cosmic scheme of things. This is true even when our questions never give way to specific answers or give rise to specific practices such as prayer or meditation.

We encounter spiritual issues every time we wonder where the universe comes from, why we are here, or what happens when we die. We also become spiritual when we become moved by values such as beauty, love, or creativity that seem to reveal a meaning or power beyond our visible world. An idea or practice is "spiritual" when it reveals our personal desire to establish a felt-relationship with the deepest meanings or powers governing life

Spiritual Practices.

Many of us want to bring spirituality into our lives but don't know where to begin. It is not necessary that we have to sit in silent meditation for an hour each day in order to be spiritual. It is better to be busy than being bored of doing nothing! Find quality time to be spent alone with you.

Focus on the breathing. A deep inspiration and holding the breath and slowly exhale. Do it as comfortable as possible- Pranayama. Have time to sit and stretch. The idea is to release tension and increase the connection to your body. Offer Pranms to the Sun god- The suryanamskara. These two processes connect the body and the mindand enjoy the Peace of mind. Sit on the ground, stand on your head. Go cross legged- all to connect the body and the mind and god.

Spirituality is being compassionate and kind, to be healthy, to be humble, do good to the society and listen to god through meditation every day after talking to him-through prayers.

Spiritual practice gives many benefits, including a calmer state of mind, increased tolerance to stress, and Bliss. You have to move from the gross to subtle. Prayer is talking to god. Pray god and submit yourself to the almighty. By praying we slowly dissolve Ego and self. This is a spiritual evolution.

One chief idea of my life . . . is the idea of taking things with gratitude and not taking things or people for granted. For me, I believe that fully experiencing and appreciating the moment with gratitude and awareness-

I start the day with a prayer simply asking that my day be filled with ease and grace. I am in awe of creation and grateful for life. Fresh air, sunshine, trees blowing in the wind, it all soothes the body, mind and spirit. I Commune with Nature. I take a long walk in the lush green ambience of my surroundings.

I meditate for twenty minutes while i perform pooja of our family deity and Mahadev. The feeling of gratitude instantly gives me perspective and moves me into a compassionate, heart-cantered space. It only takes tuning into my hardships to be utterly grateful for the things I many times take for granted such as my good health, my family, and the love, freedom, and peace in our lives. What else really matters? If you want to improve your spirituality and spiritual development, you also need to take care of your physical body: eat better. Exercise more. Breathing- I find taking a few slow deep breaths throughout the day clears my head and literally helps things flow. Stop smoking. Drink less.Live a healthier lifestyle in general.

"Thank you God for everything, I am receptive to the all good." I even try to say this in the midst of a challenge, trusting that everything is unfolding for my highest good, even when I can't see how. To Listen -I find that listening more and talking less connects me to myself and opens me up to more deeply experiencing the moment. I appreciate the person in front of me. I always greet with a -Namaste.

Non-judgment- I remind myself that we really do not know why things happen the way they do and it really doesn't matter. I try not to attach any judgment—good or bad—to how things unfold, but simply accept and experience. Whoever said "don't sweat the small stuff and it is all small stuff" is so accurate!" I keep this in mind. Letting go, is the core of trust and faith even when it appears otherwise.

Timeless truths challenging the ways of reaching Him has the integral spiritual practice evolve. It is virtually a Market place offering a bagful of choices.

Parenting can be a most powerful vehicle for spiritual growth, compassion-in-action, and evolutionary activism. Thoreau said "most men," and "most" is not "all." Who, then, are those who did not, or will not; die without fully singing the song they were born to sing? real and lasting happiness and fulfillment are an individual feelings and can only be found by going deep within, where one's essence is vividly and stunningly revealed as love -- and then living into the reality of that awareness.

Researchers have found three factors that reliably increase happiness as we grow older -- gratitude, generosity and forgiveness. Aging includes its share of reverses, losses and sorrows. What makes the difference is our attitude about them. If a bad knee means we can't jog anymore, we needn't despair; we can take up swimming. If we lost money in the recession, we can cherish what we still have. If we become ill, we rejoice when we recover.

I meditate that focuses on the positive aspects of the present, rather than regrets of the past and worries about the future. We tend to think of time as linear and horizontal, but it is also vertical -- one breath at a time. Vertical Time is really breath-based reframing the event.

spiritual practice?

Abstinence, Solitude, Silence, Fasting:, Prayer: and Meditation etc. Prayer, meditation, yoga, whirling, Tai Chi and Tantra ... these are just a few examples of spiritual practices from around the world.

Prayer is a relationship, wherein we humbly communicate, worship, and sincerely seek God's face and blessings.

In prayer we speak openly with him in Heaven. He wants us to communicate with Him through prayer. We should pray to Him. As we make a habit of approaching God in prayer, we will come to know Him and draw ever nearer to Him. Our desires will become more like His. In order to develop a clear idea of prayer, we must first have a clear idea of God. God is both universal and personal.

Prayer is not magic. He is not a genie, waiting to grant our wishes without regard for our circumstances or the consequences. Prayer is not a demand or a command. Prayer is talking to god, Meditation is listening to Him. Prayer is not for us to show off.

Breathing techniques run the gamut from simple breathing techniques to complicated rituals that involve the body, the mind and words or chants. Regardless of faith, culture or place of origin, all world religions have spiritual practices as a part of their tradition.

Fasting as a spiritual practice.

Prayer, Fasting, and Almsgiving are Spiritual Practices That Draw Us Closer to God.

Mahatma Gandhi popularized fasting as a tool of spiritual protest and in obtaining freedom. Fasting is voluntarily going without food — or any other regularly enjoyed good gift from God.

for the sake of some spiritual purpose. It is markedly counter-cultural in our consumerist society, like abstaining from physical intimacy until marriage.

The practice of fasting is self denial and cleanses of the body and be very helpful physically though most include drinking water.

One of the longest established disciplines of the human body is that of fasting. The origin of fasting as a discipline is obscure.

It is not a "little suffering" which is somehow pleasing to God. It is not a punishment which is to be sorrowfully endured in payment for sins. On the contrary, should be a joyful experience, because fasting is a self-discipline which we voluntarily done in order to become better persons.

Fasting is for this world, for stretching our hearts to get fresh air beyond the pain and trouble around us. And it is for the battle against the sin and weakness inside us. A person's entire immune system can be rejuvenated by fasting for as little as three days as it triggers the body to start producing new white blood cells, a study suggests.

Fasting can be a way to rejuvenate the body, mind, and soul. It retunes your digestive system, reduces your intake of free radicals and enhances control over yourself and your situations. Fasting is an act of cleansing, Cleansing the body, cleansing the mind, cleansing the heart, cleansing the Soul, cleansing your complete being from all the negativity that we carry within.

Today, we know that controlled fasting cleanses the body and can be very helpful physically even though most include drinking water. No fast should ever be undertaken without adequate hydration. Our body needs water on a daily basis to continue to function, whether we are fasting or not. On a strict fast, only water is necessary to continue it.

Fasts are like vacations from the pursuit of pleasure. Fasting is an aspect of diet, because diet is not only about what we are eating, but also about what we are not eating and more importantly what we should not eat. For those with a medical condition such as hypoglycaemia or diabetes, where reducing food consumption could be hazardous, a physician should be consulted before undertaking any sort of fast.

Fasting remains one of the great spiritual disciplines used by countless great sages and saints of the past. I've been determined to try it on a consistent basis in order to see if I can come any closer to enlightenment. For the past several months I've skipped midday meal. Of course i do take some fruits. Enlightenment is nowhere to be seen or felt. But i do feel attentive less drowsy and more receptive and don't need an afternoon nap.

On a basic level, my experience was simple.I stopped taking lunch and replaced it by fruits. I was a little bit more hungry than usual for week. I had no other side effects. What surprised me is that I became more interested in the practice over time. I assumed the novelty would wear off and I would get tired of it. But I liked it. I used the hunger as a way to focus myself. There was simplicity to the practice. There was a good dose of empathy as I recalled the millions who commonly get less than one meal a day as a rule. There was also a tangible sense of my body slowing down. I liked the feeling of calm and quiet that settled over me when I had no food inside.

Fasting always raises one's consciousness of the millions who go hungry every day. It makes one reflect on the geopolitics of poverty and the maldistribution of wealth, which creates enormous resentment and discontent. Fasting keeps one conscious of one's obligations toward creating a more just society and world both by personal works of mercy and promoting the common good in the social order.

Bottom line, we live in a world of abundance, and a fast can be a great guide in helping an individual understand how that richness affects us, and perhaps dulls us. I would say that after a few months of fasting, I have a little more self-control in general when it comes to food. But a fast these days does not need to be food related. The modern world has many things we can fast from: TV, phone, movies, and internet. Taking a break from anything is a healthy way for you to understand your connection to it. Absence makes the heart grow fonder, or at least grow in understanding and appreciation. I think I now have the faintest appreciation for those spiritual masters who went weeks and years with very little. I'm curious to continue to explore this practice.

Forgiveness.

I meditate to calm the mind and integrate the higher aspects of our being and to lower self ego. To keep relationship with God in good working order and life may go smoother because of it.

Disciplines train you to stay on course when the moods swing. If you don't, you drift away. The Spiritual Discipline is an inward and spiritual reality, and the inner attitude of the heart .The detachment from the confusion all around us is in order to have a richer attachment to God.

To forgive is good. It is a necessity. It heals your body, soul, mind and spirit. Forgetting is optional. To forgive doesn't mean you condone or approve of what happened. It doesn't mean that you don't seek justice. It does mean that you choose to release yourself from the emotional rollercoaster that negatively impacts your whole being. The person who hurt you may never know you did it. You're doing it for you, not for them.

I meditate for self control. You are not required to sit in isolation for hours on. Even fifteen minutes a day in a serene atmosphere may be early in the morning would be good enough. You need to keep the body fit. It facilitates meditation.

Distraction does not equal failure. Did you know that practicing some form of daily relaxation is one of the greatest gifts you can give yourself?

Practice Humility, Humour, and Humanity. People with a sense of humour can laugh at their own trials and tribulations. I open my heart to others. I want to be a friend before I look for friends. I believe in ELF-"Eat less food". Fasting has transformative and spiritual feel well effect. It's beyond doubt that one who eats less-lives longer. Fasts are like vacations from the pursuit of pleasure.

Ageless Body,

Merely being a centenarian is not the triumph of life but to achieve pure wisdom at that stage is the real aim. Human body is subject to entropy and decay but with a little effort we can have an ageless body, a mature soul, and a timeless mind that are our "links to immortality."

The concept of Ageless Body and Timeless Mind systematically, scientifically, and logically rationalizes the process of growing old, solves the mystery of aging of the biological body, eliminates the nagging fear of death, and revolutionizes the concept of 'the new old age' where people will easily live to be 100 and beyond. And all of this is packaged with a spiritual vision.

Age –Less and Live More. Look Years Younger as You Grow Older! Age is nothing but a number. Physical immortality is something that you can enjoy as long as you live. You live as long as you enjoy living.

Take command of your own health. Life is precious and an ageless body is your birthright. Search for the cure within the cause, the body itself is the best healer.

Strength does not come from physical capacity. It comes from an indomitable will.

Ageless is an adjective whose age cannot be defined, does not change, or having always existed without a beginning or an end. Anyone who has a beginning has an end. Ever since I was a kid the idea of growing old was repulsive to me. In my way of thinking, I prefer the term ageless. As anyone who knows me is aware, age to me is just a number. Even after my 62nd birthday, I felt so strongly that age was simply not going to stop me. Neither will I be able to stop age sneaking on me!

I'm now 65, and have never felt more vibrant and excited about life. **Focusing on the life force energy within is the key to agelessness. The mind is the body's most powerful anti-aging tool. You can eat right, take vitamins, but your mind comes first in staying and feeling young.** You must consciously decide not to age. **Joy, fulfillment, success and happiness simply do not have any age.**

2B or Not 2B Be Age-LESS.

Yes, we do age, but we can choose to feel good about it and "This is a Choice and an Attitude"

Ageless means to be free of the characteristics associated with age. Ageless thinking means to practice the exercise of thinking about maintaining a youthful state, both physically and mentally. The truth is that you are both: aging, we all are one breath and one wrinkle at a time. Even though you are both aging and ageless, it doesn't seem to matter what our birth certificates say -- whether we're in our 20s or 90s -- we get distracted by our thoughts and worries about how old we are.

When life is focused on being ageless, the more I forget my age, the more meaning my life has. I feel what we call 'ageing' is actually a chronic disease that we have simply accepted. I am Tired of feeling tired? It doesn't have to be that way!

What makes us old? Or more fundamentally what is old age? Body getting out of shape, weak muscles, brittle bones, sagging skin, stooping body, pot belly, creaking joints, greying hairs, balding pate and what not! Lack of confidence and overwhelming fear dominate the emotional side.

Regular exercise is the remedy for most of these ills which are interrelated to each other. Life of indiscipline is the root cause. Unless one punishes the body with regular sweat breaking exercises it will not listen to us. Nothing ages us. Ageless means to be free of the characteristics associated with age. Ageless thinking means to practice the exercise of thinking about maintaining a youthful state, both physically and mentally. The truth is that you are both: aging, we all are one breath and one wrinkle at a time. Even though you are both aging and ageless, it doesn't seem to matter what our birth certificates say -- whether we're in our 20s or 90s -- we get distracted by our thoughts and worries about how old we are.

When life is focused on being ageless, the more I forget my age, the more meaning my life has. I feel what we call 'ageing' is actually a chronic disease that we have simply accepted. I am Tired of feeling tired? It doesn't have to be that way!

What makes us old? Or more fundamentally what is old age? Body getting out of shape, weak muscles, brittle bones, sagging skin, stooping body, pot belly, creaking joints, greying hairs, balding pate and what not! Lack of confidence and overwhelming fear dominate the emotional side.

Regular exercise is the remedy for most of these ills which are interrelated to each other. Life of indiscipline is the root cause. Unless one punishes the body with regular sweat breaking exercises it will not listen to us. Nothing ages us. Ageless means to be free of the characteristics associated with age. Ageless thinking means to practice the exercise of thinking about maintaining a youthful state, both physically and mentally. The truth is that you are both: aging, we all are one breath and one wrinkle at a time. Even though you are both aging and ageless, it doesn't seem to matter what our birth certificates say -- whether we're in our 20s or 90s -- we get distracted by our thoughts and worries about how old we are.

When life is focused on being ageless, the more I forget my age, the more meaning my life has. I feel what we call 'ageing' is actually a chronic disease that we have simply accepted. I am Tired of feeling tired? It doesn't have to be that way!

What makes us old? Or more fundamentally what is old age? Body getting out of shape, weak muscles, brittle bones, sagging skin, stooping body, pot belly, creaking joints, greying hairs, balding pate and what not! Lack of confidence and overwhelming fear dominate the emotional side.

Regular exercise is the remedy for most of these ills which are interrelated to each other. Life of indiscipline is the root cause. Unless one punishes the body with regular sweat breaking exercises it will not listen to us. Nothing ages us as quickly as hearing doesn't have the energy he used to have, but he "can't expect it" at his age. It may seem logical, but it's depressing to hear such negativism..

I have decided that middle age is that point in your life when you shift from seeing the future in terms of your potential and begin to see it in terms of your limitations. It's a shift that's so slow, so incremental, that we don't even notice it on a day-to-day basis.

Middle age is the period of age beyond young adult hood but before the onset of old age.

God, middle age is an unending insult. The really frightening thing about middle age is that you know you'll grow out of it to old age with no chance of returning to young age!

Children have a lesson adults should learn, to not be ashamed of failing, but to get up and try again. Most of us adults are so afraid, so cautious, so 'safe,' and therefore so shrinking and rigid and afraid that it is why so many humans fail. Most middle-aged adults have resigned themselves to failure. There is a thing called knowledge of the world, which people do not have until they are middle-aged. It is something which cannot be taught to younger people, because it is not logical and does not obey laws that are constant. It has no rules

'Old at 60' OVER 60 WITH AIDS

Older men declare war. But it is youth that must fight and die. If the old sitting in their well cushioned offices were required to fight and die, believe me there would never be a war,

Senior citizens are riddled with AIDS -hearing aids, Band-Aids, walking aids, government aid- THE GOLDEN older YEARS HAVE COME AT LAST.

John Craven has said that the concept of ageing has changed: "Only a generation ago, many people were pretty old at 60.These days most of us in our middle and later years are much younger in our attitudes and it's all about having an active state of mind."Old age is simply a 'state of mind' - and enjoying

life to the full can keep you young. People who perceive themselves as old are more likely to quit activities which could help keep them young. The old believe everything, the middle-aged suspect everything and the young know everything

But our efforts to dodge disability appear to be falling short. Gerontologists once hoped for a compression of morbidity the idea was that we could remain healthy and active until our bodies fail at advanced ages, and we swiftly died. But new research shows that this has not materialized for most of the elderly. The price we're paying for extended life spans is a high rate of late-life disability.

The disability rate rose markedly with age. Of those who died at ages 50 to 69, only 15 percent had been very sick two years earlier. Of those who died after reaching age 90, half had been bed ridden Women fared worse. "A woman who dies at 80 has a longer period of disability than a man who dies at 80," said Dr. Ken Covinsky, a geriatrician. Women are more prone to disabling disorders like depression, arthritis or osteoporosis.

Age is an issue of mind over matter. If you don't mind, it doesn't matter. You are as young as your faith, as old as your doubt; as young as your hope, as old as your despair. Growing old is mandatory; growing up is optional. In youth the days are short and the years are long; in old age the years are short and the days long.

The years teach much which the days never knew. Inflation is when you pay fifteen dollars for the ten-dollar haircut you used to get for five dollars when you had hair. Old age isn't so bad when you consider the alternative. Sixty-five is when you finally get your head together and your body starts falling apart.

Youth would be an ideal state if it came a little later and stayed all life. Grandkids don't make a men feel old; it's the knowledge that they are married to a grand mom does! Adults over age 50 feel at least 10 years younger than their actual age, One-third of those between 65 and 74 said they felt 10 to 19 years younger, and one-sixth of people 75 and older said they felt 20 years younger. Most say old age begins at 75. Now consider the answer given by people under 30. Most of them think you're old by the time you hit 60.

In most parts of the world, women live, on average, longer than men; even so, the disparities vary between 9 years or more in countries such as Sweden and the United States. It is the beauty of youth that they do not think of their age. For them it happens. That's the time they have a narrow waist and a broad mind. The middle age creeps on them and their own lifestyle of all work and earn with no exercise the paunch makes its way. Baldness creeps in vision drops; diabetes gets its pride of place along with hypertension. That is middle age with a dash into old age

I would think that nobody need appear old with aging if you have the right diet, the right exercise, the right life style and the right attitude. Smile because your dressing if you do not wear a smile. Laugh when you are ecstatic, love one and all, be gentle to the weak, be understanding etc,

You can be the world's richest man or woman, but when the end comes, you have to leave everything behind. The end is the great equalizer of us all, the rich

and the poor. Every evil leaves a sorrow in the memory, until the supreme evil, death, wipes out all memories together with life.

Ageing is the single greatest challenge facing our society today. Recent breakthroughs have demonstrated that it is possible to combine a long life with the absence of age-related disease. Scientific advances and the consequent progress of medicine have made a decisive contribution in recent decades to prolonging the average duration of human life.

Women have the right attitude about the age and that keeps them young – at least that is what most of them think. They always remember the birth date and the month and never the year. So they are not aware of their age and they feel young.

Old age is inevitable but growing up is optional. Are all the people growing old are mature? This has been bothering me for quite some time. All are not mature and in fact many of them are silly. Yes indeed growing up is optional. Old age isn't so bad when you consider the alternative.

STAGES OF LIFE

Term	Age (years, inclusive)
Newborn	birth to 1 month
Infant	0 to 1
Toddler	1 to 2
Preschooler	3 to 4
Child/Kid	5 to 9
Pre-Teenager	10 to 12
Teenager	13 to 19
Vicenarian	20 to 29
Tricenarian	30 to 39
Quadragenarian	40 to 49
Quinquagenarian	50 to 59
Sexagenarian	60 to 69
Septuagenarian	70 to 79
Octogenarian	80 to 89
Nonagenarian	90 to 99

No doubt about it, exercise makes us sweat. Alternatively exercise with sufficient intensity and there is pouring out of sweat. Perspiration helps the body stay cool despite the increased internal temperatures produced by exercise- Literally, sweating it out.

Personally, I do not think that we have any chance of conquering death and disease and old age can be disciplined not to feel so old as you are. Differences are sometimes made between populations of elderly people. Divisions are sometimes made between the young old (65–74), the middle old (75–84) and the oldest old (85+).

The sharp decline in m mortality since 1950 and a steady recent decline in fertility have contributed to the process of population aging in India. Roughly 100,000 people worldwide die each day of age-related causes.

People are living longer. In 1970, the average life expectancy in developed countries was at birth was 70.8 years; in 2000, it was 76.9 years; and by 2030 it is estimated that the age 85 and older, could grow to 10 million people. It no longer means physical decline and illness— in the last two decades, the rate of disability among older people has declined dramatically.

Factors that not only increase longevity, but also promote what is known as "active life expectancy"—the time of advancing years free of disability. Presently the focus is on what is known to help promote healthy aging: healthy eating and physical activity.

Conventionally, there are two processes considered to be involved in the aging of a population-Aging at the base and aging at the apex of the population-The former results from a decline in fertility; the latter, mortality reduction among the elderly. In India, both processes are recent phenomena.

The number of elderly, both in absolute and percentage terms, is larger in the rural areas of India than in urban areas. Unlike the trend in most countries, there are more males than females in the elderly population for all the years.

The outer "I" wears clothes, eats, seeks and enjoys material wealth, socializes, engages in myriad other activities, "identifies with pain, pleasure, poverty, happiness, sadness, youth and old. Some people thrive under stress while some crumble. It is not the stressful event but "your inner appraisal of it and your body's reaction" that allow stress to take its toll.

The better the body is able to process oxygen, nutrients, heat generation and energy conservation, the longer he or she will live. The longer and more efficient the heart is about to regulate blood, the longer is the life. Is it possible to not only live longer but live better? Yes it is possible. Dr Chopra claims "Meditation lowers Biological Age." He writes, Transcendental Meditation is "based on the silent repetition of a specific Sanskrit hymn leads to youthful transformation.

Scientists believe that if everybody adopted a healthy lifestyle and medical advances in prevention, early detection and treatment of disease continue at their present pace, we could achieve an average life expectancy of 85 or 90. Most people have no desire for extra years that include disability and suffering.

Genetics are critical to long lives, but the best data shows that only about one-third of longevity is due to genes. We can expect women to live about five years longer than men, on average. It is difficult to tell exactly why this happens, and it is likely a result of many individual points interacting. Lifestyle affects life expectancy more than genetics,

How long your parents lived does not necessarily affect how long you will live. Instead it is how you live your life that determines how old you will get, reveals research from the University of Gothenburg recently published in the Journal of Internal Medicine. How long any of us will live is dictated, in part, by our family history. If you inherit good genes, you have a better shot at reaching old age. No surprise there. The old man Effect! But a new study conducted in the Philippines adds an interesting twist. It turns out your life expectancy may be affected by how old your grand dad was when your dad was born.

The body wears clothes, eats, seeks and enjoys material wealth, socializes, engages in many other activities, "identifies with pain, pleasure, poverty, happiness, sadness, youth and old age. We suffer from sickness, aging, and finally death.

It is common for societies to divide themselves into various age groups for the purpose of ascribing rights and responsibilities, and indeed some age differentiation can be useful such as primary education for the 'young' and pensions for the 'old'. Your life started when a sperm from your father fertilised one of your mother's eggs. About nine months later you were born: a mass of billions of cells.

There is no consummate definition of aging, but we know age when we see it. Studies have indicated the approximate age chronologically. Yet, subjective perceptions of aging based on appearances are oftentimes incorrect. My chronological age is a matter of years after my birth, my biological age is function of vital organs, my psychological age is growing, my emotional age is mature, and my functional age is young.

I have no qualms with my age. I am worried the way in which society determines who I am and what I am capable of by my number of years in existence or as they perceive it.

"You're 40, be disciplined, you can still hold on to the middle age too and you are old for extravagances

"You're 30, find a responsible job and invest in small investment plans and prepare for your retirement and pension

"You're 20, too young to worry about your health.

You are in teens and the world is at your feet and enjoy

The Cry opens the lungs, washes the countenance, exercises the eyes, and softens down the temper; so cry away. Charles Dickens.

Yes it may be good to cry at times. I am convinced that life is 10% of what happens to me and 90% how I react to it. Since adopting this as my daily mantra I no longer get angry and I'm a calmer, happier and more productive person as a result.

Genetics may not be determining your longevity. A centenarian may not have a centenarian parent. So the question is, what makes a person live for long. Your body is aging beyond your control. If there is anything natural and inevitable about the aging is that Time exists and we are captives of that absolute 'Time'. No one escapes the ravages of time.

According to Erik Erikson's "Eight Stages of Life" theory, the human personality is developed in a series of eight stages that take place from the time of birth and continue on throughout an individual's complete life. He characterises old age as a period of "Integrity vs. Despair", during which a person focuses on reflecting back on his life.

Newman & Newman proposed a ninth stage of life, Elder-hood. Elder-hood refers to those individuals who live past the life expectancy of their birth cohorts. There are two different types of people described in this stage of life. The "young old" are those healthy individuals who can function on their own without assistance and can complete their daily tasks independently.

The "old old" are those who depend on specific services due to declining health or diseases. This period of life is characterized as a period of "immortality vs. extinction." Immortality is the belief that your life will go on past ; some examples are an afterlife or living on through one's family. Extinction refers to feeling as if life has no purpose, an individual could have lived past all family and friends and feel a great loss.

In most parts of the world, women live, on average, longer than men; even so, the disparities vary between 9 years or more in countries such as Sweden and the United States.

We are all aging and getting older. You are a day older today than you were yesterday. Most people would like to be younger than their chronological age. There is nothing wrong with ageing. It is the natural process of the human body and certainly cannot be arrested. It can, however, be done gracefully with every attempt made to remain independent and productive.

Is there a right way of feeling 65? I assume there must be if so many other people are confident about stating how old they feel; but if there is, it escapes me. How should a 65-year-old feel- Happy, sad, grateful, tired, terrified, dull, hopeless, out of my depth, experienced, stupid! At times I feel all of these things.

What are Some Characteristics that Accelerated Aging- Hopelessness, depression, blocked emotions, lack of purpose in life, loneliness career problems, anger .sense of worthlessness etc

What are Some Characteristics that Invite Agelessness?

The right kind of food is next. Foods with antioxidant properties and fibre like fruits, vegetables, berries, nuts, whole unrefined grains and pulses are the best options.

Have a regular fitness routine that includes some cardiovascular activity like, running, speed walking, cycling or aerobic sessions. This should be balanced with adequate strength and muscle building

The years teach much which the days never knew. Inflation is when you pay Rs 100/- for the Rs 50/- haircut you used to get for

Rs 10/- when you had hair. Old age isn't so bad when you consider the alternative. Youth would be an ideal state and stayed all life.

New national survey on aging from the Pew Research Centre, explained the perceptions of those who participated in that survey-Most adults over age 50 feel at least 10 years younger than their actual age, the survey found. One-third of those between 65 and 74 said they felt 10 to 19 years younger, and one-sixth of people 75 and older said they felt 20 years younger. Most say old age begins at 75. Now consider the answer given by people under 30. Most of them think you're old by the time you hit 60.

In most parts of the world, women live, on average, longer than men; even so, the disparities vary between 9 years or more in countries such as Sweden and the United States. Middle-aged adults often show visible signs of aging such as loss of skin elasticity and greying of the hair. It's the time that you should start wearing walking shoes again and for some free exercises and eat less but nutritious food. Always eat with heart in mind.

Adam was created first and so there were mistakes. God created a better version rectifying all the mistakes. So the eves out live Adams. Nowadays women. outlive men by about five to six years. By age 85 there are roughly six women to every four men. At age 100 the ratio is more than two to one. And by age 122—the current world record for human longevity—the score stands at one-nil in favour of women.

In fact, the difference in lifespan has remained stable even throughout monumental shifts in society. Of course, social and lifestyle factors do have a bearing, but there does appear to be something deeper engrained in our biology," says Tom Kirkwood, who studies the biological basis for ageing at Newcastle University in the UK.

Chromosomes come in pairs, and whereas women have two X chromosomes, men have an X and a Y chromosome. Having two X chromosomes, women keep double copies of every gene, meaning they have a spare if one is faulty. Men don't have that back-up. The result is that more cells may begin to malfunction with time, putting men at greater risk of disease. Research has shown that smoking less and taking better care of their hearts are the reasons why women have benefitted more from increased life expectancy

Taller men and women are considered to be more intelligent, tough and competitive, and are more likely to be chosen for more paying jobs; it's easier for taller people to have the upper hand. Scientists have finally answered the million-dollar question: why men on average don't live as long as women/ According to a new study, men appear more vulnerable to heart disease than the inaptly-named 'weaker sex'. As a result, they succumb earlier. Statistically, women are less prone to heart disease and smoking related diseases.—which are the leading causes of death—due to making healthier lifestyles choices. Heart disease is the main condition associated with increased excess male mortality,

From middle age you have only one way – to the old age and no return. It is this inevitable fact that makes the young to refuse to accept the ageing and the baggage that comes with it. Growing old is unknown in the lives of everyone who is not yet old. You can get old and still be in great shape, physically active, and feeling good….

Healthy living doesn't happen at the doctor's office. The road to better health is paved with the small decisions we make every day. The face that looks back at me in the mirror perpetually surprises me, and I have to remind myself that others don't see me the way I see myself. On the other hand, I'm very glad that I'm not actually 26 – life is SO much better now, and I'm so much happier with myself. So getting older is kind of cool – you still feel like you're young and energetic, but you have all the benefits of wisdom and life experience.

I am 60and something and feel young. When I look in the mirror I keep wondering who that "old" person is!!! -looking at me.

I am convinced that we are going to have to stop thinking of just three ages – the first, very young and learning; the second, prime of life, working and breeding; and then the third age, old and past it – thus placing people who are senior civil servants, non-executive directors. Age is just an attitude. If you think you are old, you will get old. It's about mind over matter - if you don't mind, it doesn't matter. Age is of no importance unless you are cheese.

You can be the world's richest man or woman, but when the end comes, you have to leave everything behind. Death is the great equalizer of us all, the rich and the poor, famous and the not so famous. Every evil leaves a sorrow in the memory, until the supreme evil, death, wipes out all memories together with life.

The human race has spent millennia celebrating, damning and defying old age. But understanding it, from a scientific standpoint, has long proved elusive. Ageing is one of nature's almost universal phenomena but still one of its most mysterious.

Ageing in humans refers to a multidimensional process of physical, psychological, and social change. Some dimensions of ageing grow and expand. over time, while others decline. Reaction time, for example, may slow with age, while knowledge of world events and wisdom may expand. Research shows that even late in life, potential exists for physical, mental, and social growth and development .Ageing is an important part of all human societies reflecting the biological changes that occur, but also reflecting cultural and societal conventions. Roughly 100,000 people worldwide die each day of age-related causes.

The problem is, our absent-minded way of eating is starting to make a difference when we step on the scale -- and not in a good way. We are to what we eat and how much we eat, we are really a nation of mindless eaters, and we do not eat with heart in mind. It is easy to build up calories and it is heel of a job to burn them. The less you burn the calories get into the vessels, heart, liver and everywhere.

Always eat slowly and slightly. Don't be seduced by labels, Be satisfied with your food and eat only when you are hungry.

Timeless Mind

Timeless Mind or Does time only exist in the human mind?

Time and mind carry an inverse relationship. When not happy Time is appears to be long. When mind is happy the time appears too short! When it is unhappy the time appears too long as if to prolong the agony. On the contrary when it is happy time appears too shot as if it is envious amd to rob the joy. When is quiet times passage is normal with nothing much happening! Surely this behaviour of time must be mindless time!

The heart of the problem is time. Time is arguably our most precious non-renewable resource. It just slips out and never waits for anyone. Attention and memory also have powerful effects on time perception. Walking somewhere new seems to take longer than the walk back.

Age affects perception of the past. As people get older, and accumulate experiences, fewer activities remain novel and few are remembered in detail. Ask a busy person for 10 minutes today, and they won't have it. But ask for an hour sometime next year, and they will gladly schedule you in, even if they are.

unlikely to slow down in the interim. There was a time when time was measured by shadows.

The key to immortality is first living a life worth remembering-Absorb what is useful. Discard what is not. Add what is uniquely yours. once Bruce lee said- I fear not the man who has practiced 10,000 kicks once, but I fear the man who has practiced one kick 10,000 times. Practice makes him perfect. Consider the knowledge you already have — the things you really know you can do and perfect it. Don't quit half way.

Brain is most eager for knowledge. Ask, When? Where? How? What?" and Why? But afraid and ashamed to ask in order to get it. The question never makes the asker seem foolish or childish — rather, to ask is to command the respect of the other person. While asking, be humble. No man knows everything,

You never learn much until you really want to learn. The narrow mind stays rooted in one spot, the broad mind is free, inquiring, unprejudiced; it seeks to learn. Need is the mother of all inventions and Desire is the foundation of all learning. Respect the past, take what it offers, but don't move forwards.

You never learn much until you really want to learn. The narrow mind stays rooted in one spot, the broad mind is free, inquiring, unprejudiced; it seeks to learn. Need is the mother of all inventions and Desire is the foundation of all learning. Respect the past, take what it offers, but don't move forwards.

Teach and you will remember forever. Read to acquire knowledge. Listen and listen carefully. to acquire knowledge. Observe those who are virtuous, victorious, the rich and the famous, the losers and the vast majority who are listless and merely exist and you will know the difference. REASON and only men can reason. Reason is also known as logic. Logic is the avenue to intellectual growth and truth.

Seek to understand the root. — It is futile to argue as to which single leaf, which design of branch, or which attractive flower you like; when you understand the root, you understand all its blossoming.

The quest for intellectual growth and self-improvement through education has occupied the minds of all.

Mind creates the past and the future, the past in the memory and the future in the imagination. Time has a past tense, present tense and a future tense. We are creating and encouraging a culture of distraction where we are increasingly disconnected from the people and events around us by the technology and the gadgets. We inhibit real human connection when we prioritize our phones over people right in front of us.

We have got a crisis of attention. We are becoming a distracted culture. We are losing ourselves, of our relationships to one another and i would say our humanity. We are driven by the mobile phones. I find some carrying two mobile phones to check email, to text, to see if there are missed calls.

This constantly robs of my personal space, of solitude and solace. The mobile phone is distracting me and it is increasing all the time! This is not multitasking but doing the tasks less efficiently.

But, my favourite part about multi-tasking is that it is proven that the more you do it, the worse you are at it.

Why do most all of us seem to fall prey to these devices even as we know they're causing a real problem for us? We have got a crisis of attention, mostly caused by these devices which are with us everywhere and it is going to get worse unless we become conscious about it. It is a form of OCD- Obsessive compulsive disorder and the good news is that there are no withdrawal symptoms.

Science cannot predict the duration of a human life. Genetics, too, fails, because a centenarian may not have a centenarian parent.

The quality of your life -- for better or worse -- is determined by one thing: the level of your consciousness. There is nothing inevitable about aging--that is the inspiring message from Dr. Deepak Chopra.

I read a poem written by Rashtra Kavi Prof Shivarudrappa who says that we always look for god in the temples, churches and mosques; He is not in the brick and mortar of these monuments. He is in you – Aham Brahmosmi". He is in all the human beings, animals and this world. Sky is the limit, oceans and the vast earth, and the whole universe is His. He is limitless and eternal.

The authority of those who teach is often is an obstacle to those who want to learn.

In real time

The actual time during which a process takes place or an event occurs, something in which results, feedback, or statistical data follow input with no noticeable delay.

Even in a healthy brain, time is elastic. Staring at an angry face or keeping an angry face for five seconds feels longer than staring at a neutral one. It may be no coincidence that the pulse-generating neurons are directly wired into regions of the brain that handle emotionally charged sights and sounds.

Does it mean we its slaves. We stretch and twist it to serve our own needs. Time, in other words, is just a tool. When the mind contracts, when it is unhappy, time appears to be too long. When the mind expands, when it is happy, time appears to be too short. When the mind is in equanimity, it transcends time.

When the mind is dull or unconscious, it is unable to experience itself. When the mind is excited or happy, time seems to be too short and when the mind is miserable, time seems to be too long. To escape from the two extremes, many resort to alcohol and to sleep.

To recognize divinity, Become one with God. Do not look for God somewhere in the sky, in the temples, in the churches and the mosques, but see God in every living being, in the mountains, water, trees and finally only when you see God in yourself.

We are programmed in our day to day life. We are bound by time all the time. There are appointments and pressing deadlines. You are rushing to meet the dead lines and get stressed out. You miss the program and you are stuck in a cobweb. Be prudent in the use of time. Learn to say no to issues that are not important and those that cannot be included in your schedule. Prioritise your goals and the deadlines.

Be practical, and be able to do the best or even better than best. Remember all this is wrapped in the mystery of time. In today's day and age we can easily become overwhelmed with information. It is one sure way of getting stressed. It is this feeling of overwhelm, of not feeling capable of being able to deal with many tasks at one time, that leads to chronic stress and fatigue. The only way of this stress management is to learn the skills of Time management

Average brain contains about 100 billion neurons. Brain is the physical entity. Mind and soul are abstract. How and where are these mind and soul to be localised? Brain is the seat of mind. Soul might be in the heart or the mind. Brain is exceptionally delicate and vulnerable. The Brainstem is also equally potential in the completion of the Central Nervous system.

Modern marvels such as computerised tomography and magnetic resonance imaging of the nervous system have provided significant additional data. Functional magnetic resonance imaging now allows us to further localise function within the structure of the brain and correlate abnormalities of its structure and function.

Neurologists and neurosurgeons rank high among scientists participating in philosophical debates about what might extend beyond the physical world. They are constantly dealing with patients who have fallen into the deep hole of unconsciousness. In their attempts at restoring normalcy to bodies and minds, they also grapple with life and death. Inevitably, they ponder spirituality and the dominion of the soul. With all the distinctions they have both the neurologists and the neurosurgeons have not been able to lay bare the concepts of mind and soul.

To think about thinking, to wonder about wondering, to feel strongly about feeling strongly, to reflect upon reflection are some of the fundamental forms of human awareness. The paradox of the ego spiral - It is at once our triumph and our tragedy, for in this very human process reside equal potentials for ecstasy and anguish. the ego exists whether we like it or not. The focus is not to say we do not need the ego but to acknowledge that it exists and then separate its facilities within our mind.

Thoughts, feelings, emotions which are seen felt only in human beings. Do these constitute mind? What constitutes the soul? Is it that thanks giving part of mind constitute the soul? It is a mystery. No neurologist or the neurosurgeon has been able to crack the age old puzzle. What is it that constitutes intellect? Is soul the seat of thought process and emotions? Imagination is peculiar to humans, where does the process start and what constitutes the recognition of cognitive processes? No one knows for sure though some parts of the brain have been attributed to be the seats of those faculties;

Mind is not a physical entity. It cannot be seen or corrected by surgery. Brain and mind is not the same.

It is established that the brain, and from the brain alone arise our pleasures, joys, laughter and jests, as well as our sorrows, pains, grief's and tears. It is through the brain we think, see, hear and distinguish the ugly from the beautiful, the bad from the good, and the pleasant from the unpleasant... I hold that the brain is the most powerful organ of the human body...

Wherefore I assert that the brain is the interpreter of consciousness...' Hippocrates .It is possible that Hippocrates equates functional aspect of brain as the mind! There is a close relationship between the frontal lobes and intelligence. The amount of the Grey matter and the quality is the deciding factor.

the inferior parietal lobules and spatial reasoning and intuitions on numbers and the third interstitial nucleus in the anterior thalamus and homosexuality are a few more examples of specific areas of the brain linked to characteristics attributed to the mind. Paul Broca showed that damage to the area- Broca's area in the dominant cerebrum results in an inability to talk. Subsequent studies showed several other areas within the cerebrum that govern other aspects of speech.

The structures in the brain release the hormones or the chemicals which are responsible for the bodily functions. The effects of caffeine, marihuana and opium on the brain and mind are common knowledge. Chemicals within the nervous system, such as adrenaline, serotonin, dopamine, the endorphins and encephalon, enable and modify many functions of brain and mind and body we take for granted. Craig (2005) quotes the statement made by Steven Johnson:

Our personalities, the entities that make us both unique and predictable as individuals, emerge out of these patterns of chemical release!

Brain has been the most mapped organ in the body. The brain is the organ of the mind. The mind cannot be localised to particular areas within the brain, though the entire cerebral cortex and deep grey matter form important components.

Consciousness, perception, behaviour, intelligence, language, motivation, drive, the urge to excel and reasoning of the most complex kind are the product of the extensive and complex linkages between the different parts of the brain. Likewise, abnormalities attributed to the mind, such as the spectrum of disorders dealt with by psychiatrists and psychologists, are consequences of widespread abnormalities, often in the chemical processes within different parts of the brain.

Where does the soul reside? Is it apart of mind and brain or is the heart its residence? Or it the brain stem? Many consider it immortal, postulating the end to be the consequence of the departure of the soul from the body. What has the departure of the soul from the body to do with the stoppage of the heart? Are they one and the same? Do they occur simultaneously? Only god can answer as it has remained a secret for ages!

The mind and the soul remain fascinating enigmas. Whilst we have made some progress in our understanding of these two hazy constituents of life, much is as yet poorly understood. The spirit of enquiry that is the essence of science must stimulate us to continue our efforts at understanding it better. If, in doing so, we understand God better; this can only be to our advantage.

The study of the brain, mind and soul has engaged some of the finest intellects of yesteryears. It remains an ennobling and inspiring pursuit, worthy of all those who are dedicated votaries of science.

If we are not our physical brains, then what are we? Soul is not detectable or measurable. Then how can it be construed to be "I". There are interesting ideas floating around, but I don't think they are much more useful than word games.

Are mind and soul just the brain? Consciousness is the property of brain. Much like wetness rides on top of water. It supervenes upon the brain. In summary, we are on the journey of life. It is not a Gulliver's Travels. We are not interested in a society where people grow older and feebler but never to die. We are primarily interested in extending life and adding to the quality of life. The quality of life must be of a high standard and designed in such a way as to give people a reason for living longer. What we are envisioning is a future where old age doesn't exist as it has ever been known before. It is a future where we can grow healthier and more youthful as long as we wish. Come along, and reinvent your selves to be whatever and whomever you desire.

Suicide

Premature and voluntary end of life is a permanent solution to a temporary problem.

Voluntary premature end of life is the act of causing one's own execution. Suicide is often carried out as a result of severe depression, is a tragic event with strong emotional background and has severe after effects on the family. Suicide is the 10th leading cause of death; homicide ranks 17th. It is the second leading cause of death for 15 - 24 year olds- National crimes beareau.

Depression affects 20-25% of those who are ages 18+ in a given year. Suicide among males is 4x's higher than among females. Male deaths represent 79% of all suicides. 1 in 100,000 kids -ages 10 to 14 die by suicide each year. Suicide is the 4th leading cause of death for adults ages 18-65. The highest increase in suicide is in males 50+ (30 per 100,000). Suicide rates among the elderly are highest for those who are Divorced or widowed. (National Crimes Records.)

Over 800,000 people die by suicide every year. There is one death by suicide in the world every 40 seconds. (WHO) Suicide is an act of self-harm, sacrificing one's own life. Attempted suicide is the unsuccessful suicidal act. One does not simply decide to commit suicide; one is led to that decision by a series of prior events and decisions with a strong emotional letdown.

Many consider that to take away one's life with the knowledge he or she would be dead requires a strong will. Many consider it an act of running away from the problem, an act of cowardice! Many people have fleeting thoughts of death.

Most people who seriously consider suicide do not want to die. Rather, they see suicide as a solution to a problem and a way to end their pain. People who seriously consider suicide feel hopeless, helpless, and worthless. Suicide is not chosen; it happens when compulsion of ending life exceeds resources for coping with the events causing the compulsion.

Some people will react badly to suicidal feelings, either because they are frightened, or angry; they may actually increase the suicidal feelings instead of helping you.

But don't give yourself the additional burden of trying to deal with this situation alone. Just talking about how you got to where you are, releases an awful lot of the pressure, and it might be just the additional coping resource you need to regain your balance.

The risk for suicidal behavior is complex. Research suggests that people who attempt suicide differ from others in many aspects of how they think, react to events, and make decisions. Sometimes suicidal behavior is triggered by events such as personal loss or violence. Psychotherapy, or "talk therapy," can effectively reduce suicide risk.

The perception is that It is a is a lonely place to be for the people who suffer. World Suicide Prevention Day), on 10 September, is organized by the International Association for Suicide Prevention. The purpose of this day is to raise awareness around the globe that suicide can be prevented.

The heart-wrenching and horrible accounts of suicide bombings rarely reveal the underlying cause of the bombers' motivations. Studies across the globe suggest, the conventional wisdom that bombers are insane or religious fanatics is wrong. Individual bombers show no personality disorders and the attacks themselves are often politically motivated, aimed at achieving specific strategic goals such as forcing concessions or generating greater support.

The schools and colleges believe in conducting exams and giving marks or grades. Our brains cannot absorb all the knowledge that is out there – it is impossible. What we need are tools on how to solve problems and how to find the relevant knowledge in the big information jungle out there.. Knowledge is what you know not what you do with your knowledge or how to find new ideas.

I agree to a certain degree. I have never believed, even at the bachelor level, that exams are a solid indicator of what you know. .There is so much that we do not know, No that is not tested! Exams measure memory, NOT intellect. It is not fair to determine a 16 year old for life on a one hour exam. Your grade should be determined on your effort, your cleverness and your enthusiasm to learn. Students get over stressed and anxious that can really affect their social state and their mental state.

Yes, exams are important for you as their results influence future professional career, your social status and your self–esteem. Every person has own optimal level of worry and anxiety, which helps him/ her to achieve the best results. You must learn how to control your stress and extra anxiety for preparing for the exam.

Children are under more pressure now than 10 years ago, with testing and exams, and family break-up causing the most distress. One cannot treat cancer with Aspirin. Psychological counselling should be a part of the establishment of an educational institution.

Most children release the pressure by child's mind in Indian scene where natural development of a child is brutally crushed under 'perform at all cost syndrome' over Indian parents minds, that forces them to put unwanted stress over their children to perform at studies at all cost even distrusting the natural process of human development.

it is the combination of entrance tests and board exams that some students are finding it difficult to handle. In 2006, 5,857 students — or 16 a day — committed suicide across India due to exam stress, reported a survey. Sleepless nights, troubled thoughts, loss of appetite, rapid pulse, trembling hands - these are typical manifestations of exam fear. Recent research has shown that it affects all.

the systems of the human body: nervous, immune, cardiovascular, etc. Unfortunately, the negative influence of this phenomenon on the students' body and their psychology is underestimated nowadays. Social polls demonstrate that students perceive the exams as a "duel of questions and answers", as a "severe torture" as "intellectual and emotional overload".

Knowledge and excellence\\

It is sometimes easier to be happy if you don't know everything. I start by learning one thing really well. It's tempting to get distracted to want to learn, everything. The great thing is, many areas of knowledge are connected, so as you learn one thing well you will find yourself learning about many other things.

No matter what, don't let anyone tell you to stop learning! So many people lose this interest and curiosity, not usually by choice but rather because they don't have the energy. Take care of yourself physically, mentally, and emotionally so that your brain stays active and hungry. The desire to learn can be an asset.

"The will to win, the desire to succeed, the urge to reach your full potential... these are the keys that will unlock the door to personal excellence

Knowledge and excellence\\

Functional learning is learning with a purpose. Lifelong learning suggests that learning anything is good, regardless of immediate results. The justifications for functional learning are easy. The justification for lifelong learning isn't as obvious. Lifelong learning feels important, but when you break it down to practical reality, it is not for most people

Knowledge and excellence\\

It is sometimes easier to be happy if you don't know everything. I start by learning one thing really well. It's tempting to get distracted to want to learn, everything. The great thing is, many areas of knowledge are connected, so as you learn one thing well you will find yourself learning about many other things.

No matter what, don't let anyone tell you to stop learning! So many people lose this interest and curiosity, not usually by choice but rather because they don't have the energy. Take care of yourself physically, mentally, and emotionally so that your brain stays active and hungry. The desire to learn can be an asset.

"The will to win, the desire to succeed, the urge to reach your full potential... these are the keys that will unlock the door to personal excellence

Functional learning is learning with a purpose. Lifelong learning suggests that learning anything is good, regardless of immediate results. The justifications for functional learning are easy. The justification for lifelong learning isn't as obvious. Lifelong learning feels important, but when you break it down to practical reality, it is not for most people.

The internet is an answer machine; it doesn't help us ask better questions. It feeds the illusion that we already know everything we need to know to be well-informed. Searching the Internet Creates an Illusion of Knowledge. Information is easy, knowledge is difficult.

Did you know that the RATE of new information is DOUBLING every six months? Did you know that MOST of what you learn today will be OBSOLETE in two years? Human brains are boggled by the deluge. So are file cabinets, magnetic tapes, research papers and encyclopaedias — all bursting with billions of bits and pieces of information, none all-inclusive, none the first and last words on anything?"

Knowledge Is Power. Epistemology is the study of theories of knowledge. By 2000 there were 189,000 Internet hosts worldwide. Now just 10 years later, there are more than 43 million.

With 1.2 billion people under 15, it can be said that the world belongs to young people. But for the millions of youth in slums, the present as well as the future is grim. They die before they are five years old from pollution and easily preventable diseases. 700 million people don't even know what their rights are. They do not know if they have any rights at all! They do not even know if they have a right to live at all !

I fail to understand the exact meaning of perfection. I know for sure that in the pursuit of perfection we can attain excellence!

It is a basic feature of human life that while information is easy, knowledge is difficult. There has never been a shortage of mere data and opinion in human life. It's a very old observation that the most ignorant people are usually full of opinions.

Many of the most knowledgeable people are full of doubt. Other people are certainly sources of knowledge, but they are also sources of half-truths, confusion, misinformation, and lies.

Before the Internet, we were already awash in information. Wading through all that information in search of some hard knowledge was very difficult indeed. the Internet has created a superabundance of information today.

The more that information piles up on Internet servers around the world, and the easier it is for that information to be found, the less distinctive and attractive that knowledge will appear by comparison. I fear that the Internet has already greatly weakened our sense of what is distinctive about knowledge, and why it is worth seeking. Knowledge is verifiable and true.

The greatest enemy of knowledge is the illusion of knowledge. The possession of knowledge does not kill the sense of wonder and mystery. There is always more mystery. We are what we repeatedly do. Excellence, then, is not an act, but a habit.

Knowledge always speaks Wisdom listens. Knowledge is limited. Imagination encircles the world.

How do the excellent ones become excellent? -made famous by Plato'- whether human excellence is teachable? Or is it not teachable, Is excellence inherited? Knowledge is created by imaginative and critical thought. Or is it created? The key ingredients are both creativity and criticism. And we need error correction to get rid of flaws. With those two components, we can improve our knowledge and learn new things.

Yet in those areas of human life in which excellence has until now been achieved only by discipline and effort, the attainment of those achievements by means of drugs, genetic engineering, or implanted devices looks to be "cheating" or "cheap." We believe — or until only yesterday believed — that people should work hard for their achievements.

Nothing good comes easily. Even if one prefers the grace of the natural athlete, whose performance deceptively appears to be effortless, we admire those who overcome obstacles and struggle to try to achieve the excellence of the former

An increasing portion of modern life is mediated life: the way we encounter space and time, the way we "reach out and touch somebody" via the telephone or Internet. And one can make a case that there are changes in our souls and dehumanizing losses that accompany the great triumphs of modern technology.

The tragedy of life is that we get old too soon and wise too late. Excellence is the will to win, the desire to succeed, the urge to reach your full potential. Excellence endures and sustains if you didn't do anything until you could do everything, you probably wouldn't do anything." Many of those who know remain silent; and many of those who speak do not know'

Wealth without work

Pleasure without conscience

Science without humanity

Knowledge without character

Politics without principle

Commerce without morality

Worship without sacrifice."

— Mahatma Gandhi

People don't care how much you know but only are curious about how much you don't. In exams we try hard to find out what you know and not what you do not! I've always been passionate about living a life of excellence. Setting goals, overcoming challenges, getting results, celebrating the victories - these make living so rich and worthwhile. The quality of your life is determined by the quality of your thoughts. If you think life sucks, life will indeed suck. On the other hand, if you are set to live your best life, the paths will open up in front of.

you. Maybe it's all the 'good triumphing over evil'. No one can stop you if you have the right mindset.

The Search for Excellence that once fired the imagination of the best amongst us has been edged out. What we now celebrate is the Search for Success! Shops today are stacked with books that teach you only to win. Winning is not just everything, they warn you, winning is all. If you don't win, everything is in vain.

Winning at any cost, even by hook or crook is the goal. You can lead a race all the way but if you don't breast the tape before the rest, you don't even count for a footnote. Excellence, on the other hand, is what you spend a lifetime seeking. It's an art form, a faith. It teaches you to align yourself with the best. While success teaches you that you get only one shot at winning. Blow it, you're gone.

We forget that the winner is not always excellent. We also forget that excellence doesn't always ensure a win. . In fact, we were even taught how to lose well and gracefully. By making defeat so ignominious, we are forcing losers to lose sight of life. Courage, heroism, dignity in defeat, the power to learn from one's mistakes are all yielding way to one thing: Nothing.

Most men lead lives of quiet desperation and go to the grave with the song still in them. – Henry David Thoreau.

A willingness to go beyond one's limitations, by operating outside a level of safety and comfort is required to give a shot at excellence. If you want greatness in your life, it is not won within the circle of mediocrity. You need to push beyond this area into the level of excellence. Sing your song while you still have life to sing it! In life you should know where the goal posts are.

Do what you love; you will not do incredible things without an incredible dream. Demonstrate your positive personal values in all you do and say. Be sincere and real. Match behaviour with values. FAILURE LEADS TO SUCCESS – Learn from mistakes. Think before you speak. Make sure your intention is positive and your words are sincere. Speak honestly and kindly.

Be responsible for your thoughts, feelings, words, and actions. Own the choices you make and the results that follow. Take responsibility for actions.

Some of the world's greatest feats were accomplished by people not smart enough to know they were impossible. The woods would be very silent if no bird sang there. There ought to be so many who are excellent but there are so few. I have the simplest tastes. I am always satisfied with the best. We are what we repeatedly do. Excellence then is not an act but a habit.

When I speak of excellence I never mean extraordinariness. I mean rather the utter repudiation of mediocrity, for mediocrity is sin. In rejecting mediocrity I am not rejecting ordinariness. We should pursue excellence, but we should never aspire to be extraordinary. Extraordinary people are those who think they have transcended their humanness, think they no longer put on their trousers one leg at a time.

We must realize that we cannot be the best in everything we do. We must define what we are and what we can. We have to define what our own core competencies are. Headaches shared are headaches divided.

"Heisenberg's 'Certainty Principle'

Lesson No. 1: Be prepared for good luck. It is fleeting, and it flies away like wisps of snow in a winter storm.

Lesson No. 2: Beware of your preconceived notions. They will make you ordinary.

You cannot overestimate the wisdom bequeathed to you by your own failures or your own incompetence. Don't dwell on it, but incorporate it into your act. The adult mind is quite capable of learning from personal stupidity.

Lesson No. 3: Cherish your mistakes. It's the best feedback you will ever get.

Lesson No. 5: Seek out partnerships, but know your partner is not you.

Throughout all this, we must remember our primary responsibility—to remain honest and moral and true. This becomes an even higher goal as you move into positions of greater influence.

Lesson No. 6: Do well & Do Good. It is its own reward.

Before I summarize when the spark comes, when the opportunity arises, when you've purged your biases, when you've learned to accept your mistakes, when you know who to trust, Learn to act with not just talk but with integrity.

Look away occasionally at something outside your realm, something different, something irrelevant, and every so often you will find order, beauty, even—and if you're lucky—truth.

Education is for life. Nothing else is.

We must create processes that enable excellence. We must build a strong foundation of information technology, because in this complex, dynamic world, it is imperative that we use the most modern tools to keep processes updated.

I have found that while great individuals are important, one cannot be satisfied with pockets of excellence.

Fear Of failure.

Nothing Fails Like Success, Nothing Succeeds Like Failure. Nothing Succeeds Like Success. Develop a habit of planting trees knowing well that you will not be the one to enjoy its shade nor its flowers or fruits

It's almost impossible to go through life without experiencing some kind of failure. We can choose to see failure as "the end of the world," or as proof of just how inadequate we are. Or, we can look at failure as the incredible learning experience that it often is. Every time we fail at something, we can choose to look for the lesson we're meant to learn. Warren Buffet, one of the world's richest and most successful businessmen, was rejected by Harvard University. Richard Branson, owner of the Virgin empire, is a high school dropout.

How can you learn to use failure to your advantage, rather than dreading it. Research shows that only 20% of people achieve anything close to their true potential. Our education system and society at large reward the idea of striving for perfection: getting an "A" on an exam, flawlessly executing a project, looking like the super fit people on the cover of most magazines; and yet, in the world of entrepreneurship, perfection is more of a liability than an asset.

The best response to perceived failure is to ask oneself, What did I learn from this situation? Stay cool and anlyse. You will get the answers and you will soon be a wiser self.Fear is not real. It is a product of thoughts you create. It is what you perceive. I have been thinking about the "Fear is not real" idea. Fear is not real. Fear is a choice. Fear is distortion.

Fear is not real.

It can only exist in our thoughts,

About future events that may, or may not occur,

as a product of our imagination.

This is likening to being insane.

Danger is real.

But, fear is a choice. We are all telling ourselves a story, choosing how we respond to perceived danger, and we can change how we choose. Nothing succeeds like success. Is it not paradoxical that Nothing Fails like success. It is also true that nothing fails like failures.

Yet when you look closely, you'll find that every fear you experience is actually made of thought. It's thought appearing real.

Fear destroys creativity, hope, peace and joy. We have to commit every day to banishing fear from our lives. But a tremendous number of people live their lives paralyzed by fear. Have confidence to develop humility. Only courage can overcome fear.

Is fear really a choice? What is fear, really? Where it comes from in the first place? Where it goes when it's not there? I Indeed have no answers. A question has to have an answer.

And it is now clearer to me that we indeed have a choice, between 2 "fears" – one false, one True: that is when we worry, we are anxious, or live in fear – of anything. Well, in those moments where i recognize thought as the source of my fear. Since I don't even know what I'm going to be thinking sixty seconds from now, it's apparent to me that the vast majority of the time, I don't choose my thoughts.

And since fear is made of thought, it seems to me that the majority of the time, I don't really choose whether or not to feel afraid. Since I can at least intellectually recognize that the source of all fear is thought, I don't have to make a big deal out of being afraid.

Feel the fear and be done with it, is no doubt a phrase that you have heard uttered. You probably muttered a few choice phrases beneath your breath in response! It's easy to say this when you aren't really afraid, is probably what you were thinking.

Successful people you will generally hear them reference the fact that one of their greatest motivating forces was in fact fear of failure. Their fear drove them to work harder and leave no stone unturned. This is a great example of how a potential negative force can be turned into a powerfully positive motivating factor.

Fear is something that is triggered instinctively. It is part and parcel of our primary instinct to survive. You might say it is a primitive instinct. In fact it is so deeply embedded into our psyche that it comes upon us instinctively and automatically. We feel our bodily senses tuning up and shifting into red alert.

Thomas Edison said many of life's failures are men who did not realize how close they were to success when they gave up.

The question now is how do we foster that sense of competence in our lives that is so essential to our well-being? Competence, sometimes known as self-efficacy or our confidence in our ability, is built on earlier success. It is an upward spiral of confidence in our ability based on previous experience. It's also partly perception. When we recall the past, what do we recall? Where do we put our focus?

Never give up; you might be closer to reaching your goal than you think.

Failure refers to the state or condition of not meeting a desirable or intended objective.

Everyone fears failure. When it comes to failing, our egos are our own worst enemies. As soon as things start going wrong, our defence mechanisms kick in, tempting us to do what we can to save face. It seems to be the hardest thing in the world to admit we have made a mistake and try to put it right. Recognize when you have not succeeded. Remove emotions from the equation.

Do not get too attached to your plan. Finding a safe space to fail is a state of mind. Overcoming Fear of Failure is Facing Fears and Moving Forward. The fear of failing can be immobilizing – it can cause us to do nothing, and therefore resist moving forward.

It's almost impossible to go through life without experiencing some kind of failure. People who do so probably live so cautiously that they go nowhere. Put simply, they're not really living at all.

In order to achieve greatness, you have to fail greatly. Robert Kennedy

But breakthroughs depend on it.

Error provides the feedback that points the way to success. Only error pushes people to put together a new and better trial, leading through yet more errors and trials until they can ultimately find a viable and creative solution. To meet with an error is not to fail, but to take one more step on the path to final success. No errors means no successes either.

Forgive and may not forget.

When someone you care about hurts you, you can hold on to anger, resentment and thoughts of revenge. You have a choice, embrace forgiveness and move forward, you can also embrace peace, hope, gratitude and joy. Forgiveness is a decision to let go of resentment and thoughts of revenge. Forgiveness is giving up my right to hate you for hurting me- The act that hurt or offended you might always remain a part of your life

Forgiveness always seems so easy, when we need it, and so hard when we need to give it. Is forgiveness a conscious choice, a physical act involving the will, or is it a feeling, an emotional state of being? Forgiveness does not come easy for most of us. Our natural instinct is to recoil in self-protection when we've been injured. Is it not true that when we ask people to forgive we ask them to suffer twice: the initial hurt, and then again as they wish the one hurting them be forgiven and wish them well?

How do we forgive when we don't feel like it? How do we translate the decision to forgive into a change of heart?

We don't naturally overflow with mercy, grace and forgiveness when we've been wronged. Since forgiveness goes against our nature, we must forgive by faith, whether we feel like it or not.

We must trust God to do the work in us that needs to be done so that the forgiveness will be complete. So go ahead and play god!

Would it be easy to forgive if they apologise their act of hurting you! Does the apology have so much of power to ignite the feelings to forgive! We must manifest a life-condition of compassion to be able to forgive.

Offenses are common, and the offender usually wants to be forgiven. But the offended is usually reluctant to forgive, particularly if the offender hasn't learned anything from the ordeal. Indeed, experts say that forgiving those who have wronged us helps lower blood pressure, cholesterol and heart rate. One study found that forgiveness is associated with improved sleep quality, which has a strong effect on health.

Betrayal, aggression, and just plain insensitivity leads People to hurt us in a million ways, and forgiveness isn't always easy. Generally, forgiveness is a decision to let go of resentment and thoughts of revenge. One of the thorniest and most difficult things we humans are ever called upon to do is to respond to evil with kindness, and to forgive the unforgivable.

We love to read stories about people who have responded to hatred with love, but when that very thing is demanded of us personally, our response seems to be anger, dread or anguish, depression, righteousness, hatred, etc. Yet study after study shows that one of the keys to longevity and good health is to develop a habit of gratitude and let go of past hurts.

Forgiveness doesn't mean that you deny the other person's responsibility for hurting you, and it doesn't minimize or justify the wrong. You can forgive the person without excusing the act. Yes you forgive. Do you have to forget the issue as well?

Forgiveness brings a kind of peace that helps you go on with life. Express the emotion. Let yourself feel hurt and angry. Verbalize the way you feel. Understand why. Was it a misunderstanding? Where was the fault, with you or with the other person? If the fault was with you, you will not get hurt!

Before you forgive, you need to feel reasonably sure that the act won't reoccur. Would an apology ensure the real change of heart from the one who has hurt or caused pain? May be it depends on the gravity of the pain and hurt!

Let go. Perhaps it's the hardest part making a conscious decision not to hold a grudge. If you are in love can you forget the transgressions by the other. How would you ensure the prevention of recurrence? By letting go, you give up your role as the victim. Forgiveness is a commitment to a process of change. Then reflect on the facts of the situation, how you've reacted, and how this combination has affected your life, health and well-being.

When you're ready, actively choose to forgive the person who's offended you. Then you are not a victim and he is not an offender! As you let go of grudges, you'll no longer define your hurt relating to the act of the offender.

Go around and perfect yourself before you start judging everybody else.

Even if we're not angry, if we believe the offender doesn't deserve your forgiveness, still forgive and move on. But remember the offender and the offence. Never get into a situation with the offender and subject yourself to another issue with him. Once you have condoned move away and avoid the former offender. An eye for an eye often feels viscerally satisfying. Anger must be discharged in a way that feels satisfying. Harbouring anger on the offence may be an option. Holding a grudge does in a certain sense feel good.

There are parents who've abandoned their children, Children who've rebelled against parents, Spouses who've misbehaved with each other, Friends who've betrayed us, Strangers who harmed us or our loved ones. Or even tyrants who've killed our families? Is Hitler, for example, forgivable? Can one forgive a person without forgiving their actions? Is Stallin forgivable? The question is whether they can be excused even being in full knowledge of their crime and nature of their deeds. Can their deeds be excused or forgiven?

Forgiveness doesn't mean that you deny the other person's responsibility for hurting you, and it doesn't minimize or justify the wrong. You can forgive the person without excusing the act. Forgiveness brings a kind of peace that helps you go on with life. Not always of course-But sometimes. And if it does, in forgiving them you're not only setting yourself free, you're actually contributing to something of greater importance, something the world is literally crying out for peace.

Sometimes, events that happen in our life make us feel tired, burdened, or regretful. Well think if you can undo it! You may not be able to change or undo! Accept that it happened. It's not the easiest thing to do, but it will help you get on your way. The past is a part of your life now, but it is not the most important part. Accept the fact that it can no longer be changed in any way. Learn from it and move on in life. Find the lesson and do not repeat the mistake.

To forgive is it a must for the offender to come ask forgiveness? Only When They Come to Me First and ask my forgiveness, will I ever forgive them. Never, until then, for the unkind things they had done. No- let not ego stifle your inherent goodness. In a way the act of not forgiving is to letting them control us. By thinking bitter thoughts about them we are not free of them.

For extra happiness, we want to be in control of our thoughts, not others. The offender might rarely think about us or they might be dead, so they aren't the ones emotionally suffering, we are. By not forgiving we are hurting ourselves, not them. Without forgiveness life is governed by an endless cycle of resentment and retaliation.

Forgive Yourself.

How to forgive yourself Right Now?

Accept yourself and your flaws. Know that despite your flaws, you are okay as you are. Be gentle first with yourself if you wish to be gentle with others.

Can you ever forgive yourself—no matter what you've done? Amazingly, the biggest obstacle he's found to self-forgiveness may be the tendency we have to wallow in our own guilt.

Forgiving yourself can be much harder than forgiving someone else. When you're carrying around a sense of blame for something that has happened in the past, this bundle of negativity burrowing deep into yourself can cause a never-ending, pervasive sense of unhappiness. Forgiving yourself is an important act of moving forward and releasing yourself from the past. It's also a way of protecting your health and general well-being. Here are some suggestions on how to forgive your own self.

Living in a state denial and of being unable to forgive requires a lot of energy. You are constantly chewed up by fear of your vulnerability and guilt. This energy deserves to be put to better use, so that your creativity and abilities are fed, not your negativity. Forgiveness also allows you to live in the present instead.

of the past, which means that you can move into the future with a renewed sense of purpose focused on change, improvement, and building on experience rather than being held back by past hurts.

Forgiving is often a conscious decision to let go of the pain, anger and bitterness arising from hurtful situations, then move on and live our lives the best we can despite the past. Forgiveness can take time and it can be difficult, but it's essential for boosting happiness, mental and physical health. Forgiveness is a funny thing; it warms the heart and cools the sting."- William Arthur Ward Forgiveness does not change the past, but it does enlarge the future."- Paul Boese.

Old order gives way to new.

Change is the universal law of Nature. Change is the law of progress. Nothing remains nor can remain in the same state forever. The world of Nature and man is constantly passing through changes. If we observe a river, we shall find that there is current in it and that the water is constantly changing. If this were not so, the water would be bad and unfit to be used. It is the current that makes the river flow and remains useful.

We also see that there is sunshine but this sunshine is never constant. It is followed by clouds. Clouds are followed by rain and after the rain there is sunshine again. Often you may see the Rainbow. Rain bow is not constant. Similarly, we find spring followed by summer, summer by autumn and autumn by winter. It is the same case with things human.

If variety is the sauce of life, change is the law of nature. The nature gives seasons. From morning to night, as from cradle to the grave, is but a succession of changes so gentle and easy that we can scarcely mark their progress. The process of change and challenge is always at work. For some change brings cheer, whereas for others it may mean moments of chagrin. Both painful and pleasant, a shift from the established order to a new one is inevitable. There is no monotony.

The breakup of joint family system in India is a case for study and a standing example of change that has overtaken us so fast. The emergence of nuclear family is a telling tribute to the process of change over which we have no control whatsoever. That the Indian society is at the crossroads is not a matter of fiction, but a vigorous reality.

The glamour and glitter that we see around is the result of consistent and conscious efforts that have gone into the making of 'changing patterns of society' everywhere under the sun. Change is not made without inconvenience, even from worse to better."
—Richard Hooker.

As social beings we get so attuned to old customs and conventions that it takes a lot of persuasion and even pressure to adjust to the new realities that time throws up.

The evil practices of un-touchability, child marriage, denial of education to females, etc. were some of the sore points of our social fabric that had to be changed, rather rooted out with legislation. Though healthy in intent and inclination, the change from worse to better does cause inconvenience and irritation to diehards and rigid mindsets.

Just as social ethos undergoes periodic changes, so do institutions that human beings create from time to time. If the Secretary General of the UN (Kofi Annan) advocates the need to re-invent the United Nations and its various agencies, he is not off the mark. Life is ever changing. Knowledge increases ideas. Old ideas are broadened and the vision of life is widened. To meet the growing need of life, new institutions must spring up. Whatever outlives its utility is dead. Bliss, as the poet nicely put it, was in that dawn to be alive.

There is no moral authority any more in the society. There is no ethics in public life. Even the rule of law ia not applicable one and all. Almost every day, headlines tell of the disgrace, downfall, imprisonment or forced resignation of a political, corporate, religious, or community leaders everywhere.

"Until the reality of equality between men and women is fully established and attained, the highest social development of mankind is not possible," This challenge to full equality does not ignore natural differences between the sexes.

On the subject of our nation's enemies,

President Abraham Lincoln once commented, "The money powers prey upon the nation in times of peace and conspire against it in times of adversity. It is more despotic than a monarchy, more insolent than autocracy, more selfish than bureaucracy. It denounces, as public enemies, all who question its methods or throw light upon its crimes. I have two great enemies, the Southern Army in front of me and the bankers in the rear. Of the two, the one at my rear is my greatest foe."

What personal values and beliefs will sustain you though a crisis? Does a huge change shake your faith or make it stronger? Does it make you search for answers? Life-changing events cause each of us to review our priorities and our values, and adapt or change those that do not help us through the event. Huge changes in our world can cause temporary changes in how we express our values that end when the event or the threat from the event ends. It is also amazing how we each have our own resiliency. Some of us are able to 'bounce back' more quickly than others. I believe that our resiliency depends on the type of change and how much the change has an effect on your daily life. It also depends on our age and where we are in our life.

Change is constant, even big change. But it is all a part of life and we can all learn and grow from it. And we can all help each other through. If a young child experiences an event that is beyond his or her skill level, he or she needs an adult to help learn new coping strategies or adapt a current skill.

Men & Women – equal but different!

Are men and women equal? Are XX and XXY equal? If different why and in what? Have the Indian women come out of their shells. Are they competing with men? Are they being educated? Well all these questions are important and very pertinent.

In the U.S., there are more male CEOs. Women are a minority in the Senate and the House. (Male- 80% and female 20 %.) And so is it in India. Many Women are likely to experience domestic violence (One in four)

Women are more likely to be living in poverty. Nearly six in ten poor adults are women, and nearly six in ten poor children live in families headed by women. Poverty rates are especially high for single mothers,

Women are more likely to be sexually assaulted. Women are far more likely to be the victims of human trafficking. More than 800,000 people are trafficked across international borders every year.

Pay inequality is real. For black and Hispanic women, the rates are even worse.

Women Deputy Editor, The Huffington Post

Only 41 Nobel Prizes to women!

41 Nobel Prizes and Prizes in Economic Sciences have been awarded to women and 765 to men between 1901 and 2009.

After thousands of years of male dominance, we now stand at the beginning of the feminine era, when women will rise to their appropriate prominence, Men and women are not equal -- they are different. Like apples and oranges. Man was designed to go out and be responsible for the needs of family members at home. And Women were supposed to shoulder more of the household burden.

Man and woman represent two forms of divine energy and its manifestation. The masculine form is more aggressive, and the feminine form, is more subtle. All men and women must be themselves, realizing that God has given each of us unique abilities with which to pursue our goals.

'Equal and same' are fuzzy terms when used outside of mathematics, especially when applied to people more specifically to male and female. What most of us mean by them is that men and women should be given the same opportunities, such as being offered the same jobs, assuming the same skill level; being payed the same amount, assuming the same quality of work; and given the same ability to live a life free of fear and harassment.

I simply cannot accept that women be treated as commodities. I simply cannot accept that in a country like India, woman get gropped in broad daylight with not one man putting a stop to it. I simply cannot accept that in countries like Afghanistan, it is illegal for young girls to learn to read and write. I simply cannot accept that in my country, women still, to this day earn on average 20 % to 30 % less than their male counterparts in the same type of employment. From a common sense point of view, all living creatures should be treated with respect. Is that so difficult to understand ?

Others argue that how can there be equal rights for fundamentally different people?

Men are a huge part of the problem and women as it stands at this point in time, simply do not have the power to do anything about it. Women are as intelligent, dedicated, and capable as men. When will our Constitution, and our pay checks, prove it?

God has given the supreme power of generating life and nurturing it with in the womb for nine months. It is the god Brahma who is involved with creation. God has given that supreme power to the woman. Man cannot get pregnant and conceive or nurture a life with in his body. What a difference. How can man and woman be equal and Working like A Man Does Not Make Women Equal to him? In the sexual act even if the woman were to lie on the man she cannot make him carry! Man is within WO-MAN and He with i S-HE. So woman is on a pedestal when compared to a man.

I never understood the saying "men are from Mars and women are from Venus" until I grew up and my eyes were opened to the differences between men and women. It's incredible how I didn't see them before since they're so polar opposite and incredibly attractive. I realised that a girl always chooses a man who loves her and it is not necessary for her to have loved him. A boy always chooses a girl whom he loves though the girl may not be liking him, forget loving him.

Sushmita Sen, India's first Miss Universe, The origin of a child is a mother, a woman… She shows a man what loving, caring and sharing is all about" Said in the final round of the contest. An answer which was greeted with tremendous applause and which probably, led her to win the crown.

India-born astronaut Kalpana Chawla's birth anniversary is being celebrated as 'Daughter's Day'. Yes 'Daughters do us proud'.

It is my position that men and women are equal but different. When I say equal, I mean that men and women have a right to equal opportunity and protection under the law. The fact that people in this country are assured these rights does. Not negate my observation that men and women are at least as different psychologically as they are physically.

Who is the ideal woman? In pursuing equality- when they are in fact superior, I believe women have lost something special. Perhaps women have traded too much of their femininity for equality -although we can still have equality without losing femininity. Women's emancipation has become synonymous with being like men and doing everything they do. More women who want to avoid becoming 'slaves of the family' are now becoming slaves of corporate entities and feeling trapped inside offices. Previously they were trapped at what we call homes.

In spite of all the 'liberation', more women are left wondering why happiness is still a mirage, and satisfaction nowhere in sight. India should be prevented from becoming an anti-marriage, anti-family, fatherless 'welfare state'. Laws and policies must be based on principles of equity and fairness. Women should be encouraged to inculcate self-esteem.

Women are a heady mix of sensuality and nurturing; naughtiness and caring; exuberance and quietude; palliative and intoxicating. Women are women and we are proud of them. But in pursuing equality- when they are in fact superior, I believe women have lost something special.

Women are still walking on the road to freedom. The end is not in sight. But women have grown in stature, women have grown and grown secure enough to fight as equals and can even fight for their brother's right if need be.

Women are a serious economic force to be reckoned with. Globally, women account for about $20 trillion spent annually on consumer goods; 85 percent of all consumer purchases are made by women, and women represent the majority of the online market. Seventy percent of all US and UK wealth is owned by the over 65s (who are mostly women) and it is estimated that female millionaires will outnumber male ones in the UK by 2020. By 2025, women will control 60 percent of the nation's private wealth. World Bank figures.

To-day women do all that men do and do it better in many fields like education, economics, health care etc. They are heading governments, business houses, industrial institutions and are holding senior offices in the police, bureaucracy, military, medicine, judiciary, scientific, educational institutions.

Equality is not something that can be claimed or asked for - it should exist, and when it exists there is nothing to be asked for. You can never pit woman as man's equal as long as you make her fight in an area of man's strength.

Being other than equal do not mean one is inferior or superior to the other. The progress of a society can only be achieved when men and women respect each other and co-exist peacefully to move ahead together. The rogue elements in society shall always be there and a civilized society should find rational means to deal with such untoward characters without plunging into generalizations! The bottom line is to treat all human beings with respect at all places and at all times.

Women are physically weaker and the resultant vulnerability is the villain during assault on modesty. Normally men are not raped, Women have innate self-restraint. Excepting reproductive organs, both genders are the same as human beings. Respectability too is same. Only on the plain of physical strength, fair sex is often the weaker sex. Ways should be explored to improve them to be on par with the male. The question of change of mind set is a long and cumbersome way if not a secondary issue. Indian culture is right. Vedic period had respected women and had accorded equal and superior status.

Males, Females and Humans

Humans are born with 46 chromosomes in 23 pairs. The X and Y chromosomes determine a person's sex. Most women are 46XX and most men are 46XY

For centuries, people have clung to the belief that there's something inherently different between the male brain and the female brain. While there are some distinct brain differences between men and women, there's no such thing as a distinctly 'male' or 'female' brain.

Broadly speaking, there are two different brain types. There are empathisers, who are good at identifying how other people are thinking or feeling, and there are systemisers, people who are more interested in trying to take apart and analyse systems

We are all a mix of the two, but most of us are more one than the other. Men tend to sit more along the systemising end of the spectrum, women at the empathising end, though there are plenty of exceptions.

Society would answer, Men and women are different in different ways, but all humans have things that differ between them. When it comes down to it, we are all humans and no one gender is greater than the other.

Women and men aren't as different as you might think.Mars-Venus sex differences appear to be as mythical as the Man in the Moon. A 2005 analysis of 46 meta-analyses that were conducted during the last two decades of the 20th century underscores that men and women are basically alike in terms of personality, cognitive ability and leadership.

But then you always make a rough draft before the final masterpiece. Women need love and attention from her man.

You need to give lot of time to listen to your partner. Adam was created by god, later eve was created as a companion and to converse. God blessed them together to own this earth. Today she is not the person she used to be.

Even the male has undergone distortions and is not the one created by god the Adam. Both suffer from distortions of gender that limit their ability to give one another the love and help they were made to give.. Both reflect as caricatures of the original.

Ego is very much with the male. They are vulnerable to hurt. Females are more empathetic and strong emotionally. Men have a selective memory. Once the deal is set they have a loss of memory for birth days and anniversaries which land them in lot of difficulties. Before the marriage men are perfect in remembering all the details. They love hanging around with smart women in the town, but when it comes to meeting mom, it's a homely Desi girl they start hunting for.

If you are man, be rich! Looks are of secondary importance. If you have looks in addition it is a bonus. A woman has to be beautiful. As a man you are required to Earn more than what your wife can spend. This particular gender bias sucks men into some uniquely convoluted knots..

In 1980, the United Nations summed up the burden of this inequality: Women, who comprise half the world's population, do two thirds of the world's work, earn one tenth of the world's income and own one hundredth of the world's property.

The achievement of full equality between the sexes is essential to human progress and the transformation of society. Inequality retards progress of civilization itself. Men seek youth and beauty, while women focus on wealth and status/

I am strong because I can carry my own weight-

YOGA

For enlightenment you have to light your own lamp.

Yoga is integrated Science! Taming the Body and mind is yoga!

The steady holding of the senses is Yoga!

Synthesis of life and living is yoga/ Yoga brings tranquility to an agitated mind!

Yoga is the supreme gift of India to the world at large. Yoga does not quarrel with science; it supplements it. Yoga is a methodical way to attain perfection, through the control of the different elements of human nature -both physical and psychical. Yoga is the supreme science of contacting reality. It is perfection in action. It is equanimity of attitude. It is perfect peace. Yoga is union with God.

Through yoga you can also have increased energy, vigour, vitality, longevity and a high standard of health. Yoga is a healing system. it's a combination of breathing exercises, physical postures, and meditation, practiced for over 5,000 years.

References

ESV Text Edition: 2011- The Holy Bible, English Standard Version®

www.usccb.org › Beliefs and Teachings › What We Believe, Life and Dignity of the Human Person.

How to Heal Naturally?
MEANING OF LIFE, Life Positivehttps://www.lifepositive.com/meaning-of-life-1/

Steven Jonathan Rummelsburg- Three Perspectives on the Human Person.

- Ambrose Redmoon- sophia.smith.edu/...is...ambrose-redmoon/comment-page-
- study.com/.../what-are-personality-traits-characteristics-
- Mythology - Religious views of humility - Philosophical views of humility
-Life and God - Is God real? - liferocks.org, www.liferocks.org/
- Success Is Never Final and Failure Never Fatal quoteinvestigator.com/2013/09/03/success-fina
-Quote by Captain Jack Sparrow: "The problem is not the ...www.goodreads.com/

-https://www.biblegateway.com/passage/
-Understanding Brain, Mind and Soul: Contributions from ...

www.ncbi.nlm.nih.gov › NCBI › Literature › PubMed Centra
-www.goodreads.com/autho, The 21 Irrefutable Laws ...
- https://en.wikipedia.org/wiki/Sorrow, Synonyms for sorrow at
Thesaurus.com with free online thesaurus, antonyms
- Psychology Today
https://www.psychologytoday.com/.../time-heals-all-wounds-or-
does-i
- David A. Nachtigall

www.isfma.com/.../the-two-sides-of-self-defense-perfect-and-
imperfect

- elitedaily.com/life/motivation/failures-to-make-want...in-life,
- Confucius – Wiki quote https://en.wikiquote.org/wiki/Confuciu
- The Buddhist Concept of Impermanence - Urban Dharma
www.urbandharma.org/udharma8/imperm.html

- Stolen-wealth theory does not explain global wealth ...
www.taipeitimes.com/News/editorials/archives,

Evidence for Creation › Evidence from Science › Evidence from
the Life Sciences › Man Was Created by God» Viral Genome
Junk Hits the Trash.

Connecting Character and Conduct - Cornerstone Values...
www.cornerstonevalues.org/conduct.html.

Philosophy, www.allaboutphilosophy.org/why-am-i-here.ht

Moral Dilemmas – Listverse, listverse.com/2007/10/21/
top-10-moral-dilemmas/

Faultless www.thefreedictionary.com/faultless

Purpose of Life - Why are we born, where do we come from?
www.happyscience-na.org

Time and Timelessness—A Balancing Act to Live in the ...
www.corelight.org'

To continue to exist or happen - www.macmillandictionary.com/
thesaurus.

Natural Reasons Why Life Is Hard | Psychology Today
https://www.psychologytoday.com/

Thesaurus.com www.thesaurus.com/browse/inexperienced

Answers in Genesis
https://answersingenesis.org/apologetics/critical-thinking
Life is Too Short Not to Appreciate www.marcandangel.com/.
The Meaning of Life - Spiritual Life - slife.org
slife.org/the-meaning-of-lif

What is the importance of money in one's life? Can money ...
https://www.quora.com
Turning Toward Well-being Naturally
www.wellbeingalignment.com

Letter Count / Character Count
www.lettercount.com/

Learning to forgive heal & bless, www.livingmiraclescenter.org
Bosons and bankers: What's up, God?
readersupportednews.org/pm

Fasting as a Spiritual Practice - Reality Sandwich
realitysandwich.com

Ageless Body, Timeless Mind: The Quantum Alternative ...
www.amazon.in/Ageless-Body

How Old Is Old Age? - The New York Times

well.blogs.nytimes.com

What is Real Time? Webopedia Definition

www.webopedia.com

Consciousness: Are 'we' our brains? - Quora

https://www.quora.com/Consciousness-

Suicide - Wikipedia, the free encyclopedia

https://en.wikipedia.org/wiki/Suicide

IDEAS - Knowledge of Excellence
schoolofselfawareness.org/index

Education for Life Home - Education for Life
edforlife.org.

Overcoming Fear of Failure - Career Development From ...

www.mindtools.com

Male Menopause Symptoms, Treatments, Causes, and More

www.webmd.com

Yoga - Wikipedia, the free encyclopedia

https://en.wikipedia.org/wiki/Yog

About me...

Dr. N. Prabhudev

Former Vice Chancellor Bangalore University- One of the biggest universities in India with 650 affiliated colleges and 325,000students)

Former Chairman, Karnataka state Health Commission, Government of Karnataka Bangalore

2. 3. Former Director sri Jayadeva Institute of Cardiology Bangalore(700 bedded superspeciality hospital)

As the Vice-Chancellor of the prestigious Bangalore University (2009-2013).

I was selected for the prestigious post of Vice-Chancellor of Bangalore University.

- During my tenure-, Bangalore University was ranked 13th amongst all the Universities in India Vide India To-Day, Neilson survey2010
- Again in 2011- Bangalore University was ranked 9th among all the universities in India (India To-Day Neilson survey).

- For the first time in the history, Bangalore University occupied the prestigious position of being one among the top ten universities in India.

I have played a major role in this singular achievement.

I as Vice Chancellor instituted a Central facility for scientific research with 18 Bangalore based National scientific institutions for research and hands-on experience for the teachers and students of Bangalore University.

I also instituted a Research council to award and monitors the projects with the financial allocation at under graduate, post graduate and faculty levels. He was instrumental in starting foundation day lecturers along with Indian Society for Socio-economic change. (ISEC). I Started BU-ISEC social science talent search scholarship.

After completion of my term as Vice Chancellor of Bangalore University, I was appointed as the Chairman of Karnataka State Health Commission.

During his brief period as chairman, I wrote to the Government that even after 64 years after independence there is no right to health care and that Article 47 makes improvement of public health-a primary duty of State.

I had suggested that Allocation of health budget as block funding on a per capita basis for each population unit of entitlement as per norms. He believed that this will create redistribution of current expenditures and reduce substantially inequities based on residence.

I believe that India is in a state of epidemiological transition from communicable disease state to a state of lifestyle diseases and believes in strong state supported health care mission.

Although the health insurance market covers just 10 percent of the population, it has helped growth of the private sector by free market economy. Unfortunately, the remaining 90 percent of the population remains outside the scope of the above coverage. I strongly believe in universal health coverage.

General Info

Name	: Dr. N. Prabhudev
Nationality	: INDIAN
Date of Birth	: 22nd September 1950
Place of Birth	: Srinivasapur, Kolar District
Career Record	: Chairman, Karnataka state Health Commission From 16.11.2012 for about a year
	: Vice-Chancellor, Bangalore University, Bangalore From 2009 to 2012-(4yrs)
	Director of Sri Jayadeva Institute of Cardiology, Bangalore From 1996 to 2005 —(10yrs)
	Professor & Head of the Department of Cardio-Thoracic Surgery (From 1985 to 2005)
Mailing Address	No.88, 'Classic Orchards', Bannerghatta Rd Behind Meenakshi Temple, Bangalore – 560076 Tel : Mobile : 94480 67890 080-26487890,
e-mail	nprabhudev@gmail.com contact@nprabhudev.com.
Area of Practice	: Now not active in surgery. Practice is confined to consultation
Cardiovascular & Thoracic Surgery	(General Surgery, surgical specialties)
	Higher Education- Presently on several committees and sub committees on higher education

Academic Qualification

Post Doctoral Degree	M.Ch in Cardiovascular & Thoracic Surgery	1978-1980
Post Graduation in General Surgery	MS in General Surgery (Victoria Hospital Bangalore Medical College)	1974–1976
Medical School Education :	M.B.B.S. (Bangalore Medical College, Bangalore)	1968–1972
	Compulsory Rotating Internship (Combines Hospitals of Bangalore Medical College)	1 year 1973
	Senior House Officer Dept. of Cardiology, Victoria Hospital	1 year 1974
Pre Medical Education	Pre University (St. Joseph's College Bangalore)	

Publications and presentations.

225 presentations in national and international conferences.

I performed the first open heart surgery in Jayadeva instituteof cardiology in the state of Karnataka.

I was deputed to GUY's hospital London UK for advanced training in coronary heart Bypass surgery for a year in 1985.

I had the privilege of Commissioning and dedicating to the nation the now 150 crore -700 bedded, super-specialty hospital with 7 operation theatres and 5 cardiac catheterization labs with an outpatient attendance of 125,000 patients annually, where 2500 angioplasties are done annually and nearly 2000 open heart surgeries are performed successfully.

I have been a medical teacher of 35 yrs - as lecturer, assistant professor, professor and head of the department of super-Specialty Cardiothoracic and Vascular surgery.

I have the experience of operating on more than 10,000/ open heart surgeries and over 1000/ cases of Thoracic and vascular cases in his academic career.

I have trained more than 50 cardiac surgeons

I was the president of the All India Association of Cardiothoracic Surgeons.

I was president of the association of Indian college of Cardiology.

Orations

Prestigious Sadashivam oration
PM Nayak memorial CSI oration.

Orations

Dr. Prabhu Dev has given the Prestigious Sadashivam oration of the AICTS. He has also given the equally prestigious PM Nayak memorial CSI oration.

Awards:

1. Honorary degree of the association of Cardiothoracic surgeons,
2. Honorary degree of Indian College of cardiology,
3. Karnataka State Rajyothsava Award,
4. Prestigious Karnataka jyothi award,
5. Prestigious Kempe Gowda Prashasthi of the BBMH -Bangalore city corporation with a gold medal and a citation and
6. Rani Chennamma award with citation.

Curriculum vitae. Dr N Prabhudev.

- Born on 22/9/1950 at Srinivasapur of kolar district in the state of Karnataka.

As Director Of Sri Jayadeva Institute of Cardiovascular sciences and research- A State Government autonomous super speciality Hospital.

I had the privilege of Commissioning and dedicating to the nation the now 150 crore -700 bedded, super speciality hospital with 7 operation theatres and 5 cardiac catheterization labs with an outpatient attendance of 125,000 patients annually, where 2500 angioplasties are done annually and nearly 3000 open heart surgeries are performed successfully. - I was the Director of Sri Jayadeva Institute of Cardiovascular sciences and research for nearly 10 years before I took voluntary retirement to become the VC of BU.

- I have been a teacher for 35 yrs - as lecturer, asst professor and as a professor and head of the department of Cardiothoracic and Vascular surgery at SJICS& RC.

- I have the experience of operating on more than 10,000/ open heart surgeries and over 1000/ cases of Thoracic and vascular cases in my academic career.

- My entire service as a cardiac surgeon is in the state government SJICS& RC-. This is the only hospital which undertakes open heart surgeries for the poor in the state of Karnataka.

I have presented over 210 papers in various National and international conferences.

- I started the open heart surgery program at Jayadeva Institute and the state of Karnataka.

- I performed the First open heart surgery on a Pregnant women and standardized the techniques to preserve the foetus when the heart of the mother is stopped for conducting surgery to rectify the anomaly.

- I have to my credit more than 400 cases of awake cardiac surgeries.

- I have trained more than 50 cardiac surgeons who have been conferred with MCH degree at the institute.

- I am the university examiner for various universities including central and state universities for the super speciality cardiac surgery course.

- I was the general secretary and the president of the All India association of Cardiothoracic surgeons.

- I have been the president of the association of Indian college of cardiology.

Orations

Prestigious Sadashivam oration of the AICTS
PM Nayak memorial CSI oration.
Professor Hanumaiah surgical oration

Awards

- honorary degrees of the association of Cardiothoracic surgeons
- honorary degree of Indian College of cardiology.
- Karnataka state award -Rajyothsava day award.
- prestigious karnataka jyothi award
- prestigious Kempegowda prashasthi of the -Bangalore city corporation with a gold medal and a citation.
- Rani Chennamma award with citation.

As the Vice-chancellor of the Bangalore university-2009-2013,

During my tenure as VC in 2010, BU was placed 13th amongst all the Universities in India (India-To Day Neilson survey)

In 2011- BU was placed in the 9th position (-India To Day Neilson survey).

For the first time in the History of BU it had broken into top ten universities in India. I am privileged to have played a small but significant role in this achievement.

As VC I Instituted a Global centre for foreign languages at BU.

- I got a new Ordinance passed to codify procedures and ensure transparency in the conduct of examination and announcement of results and issue of marks cards.

Instituted Examination Adalat to hear the students, parents and colleges to redress the examination related long pending issues.

As VC I Initiated UNILINK - linking the libraries of all the state Universities for better academic excellence and book sharing amongst the students and faculties in the state.

Initiated a nutritious midday meal program to support the students and possibly treat malnutrition amongst the students.

.MOU

For the first time a Central facility for scientific research with 18 Bangalore based National scientific institutions for research and hands-on experience for the teachers and students of BU was started by me In BU.

Instituted a Research council to award and monitor the research projects with the financial allocation at under graduate, post graduate and faculty levels.

Instituted foundation day lecturers along with Indian Society for Socio-economic change.(ISEC)

and Started BU-ISEC social science talent search scholarship.

As Chairman

Karnataka state Health commission –(For less than a year.)

I reminded the Govt that even after 65 years after independence there is no right to Health care. The Constitution directs the state to take measures to improve the condition of health care of the people.

Article 47 makes improvement of public health a primary duty of State. Hence, the court should enforce this duty against a defaulting authority on pain of penalty prescribed by law, regardless of the financial resources of such authority.

Allocation of health budgets as block funding, that is on a per capita basis for each population unit of entitlement as per existing norms. This will create redistribution of current expenditures and reduce substantially inequities based on residence.

Today urban areas do have adequate number of beds (including private) at a ratio of one bed per 300 persons but rural areas have one bed for 2400 patients.

The 344 medical colleges that we have established are all located in urban areas where only 25 - 30 % of the population lives. We train 38,349 doctors annually and only 20,000 nurses, The systems of a 3-tier graded health care service have been lost.

Although the health insurance market covers just 10 percent of the population, it has helped growth of the private sector by free market economy. Unfortunately, the remaining 90 percent of the population remains outside the scope of the above coverage.I have strongly recommended that state govt should introduce Universal heath coverage.

Printed in the United States
By Bookmasters